Good Choice!

SUPPORTING INDEPENDENT READING AND RESPONSE K–6

TONY STEAD

Foreword by David Booth

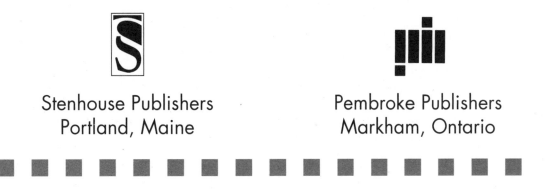

Stenhouse Publishers
Portland, Maine

Pembroke Publishers
Markham, Ontario

Stenhouse Publishers
www.stenhouse.com

Pembroke Publishers
www.pembrokepublishers.com

Credits
Page 97: *The Great White Shark* by J. Hirsch, copyright © 2006 by The Rosen Publishing Group, 29 East 21st Street, New York, NY 10010, and reprinted with permission.

Library of Congress Cataloging-in-Publication Data
Stead, Tony.
    Good choice! : supporting independent reading and response, K–6 / Tony Stead ; foreword by David Booth.
    p. cm.
    Includes bibliographical references and index.
    ISBN 978-1-57110-732-9 (alk. paper)
    1. Reading (Elementary) I. Title.
    LB1573.S826 2008
    372.4—dc22
                        2008027672

Cover, interior design, and typesetting by Martha Drury

Manufactured in the United States of America on acid-free, recycled paper
15 14 13 12 11 10 09   9 8 7 6 5 4 3 2 1

To my wife, Jennifer, and my mother, Patricia, both of whom nurtured a love of reading in their sons

Contents

Foreword by David Booth   *vii*

Acknowledgments   *ix*

Part One: Making Time for Independent Reading   1

1. Establishing Independent Reading and
    Borrowing Routines   3

2. Independent Reading Throughout the Day   23

Part Two: Providing Resources   37

3. Establishing the Classroom Library   39

4. Nonbook Resources   55

5. Independent Reading and the Computer   69

Part Three: Providing Support   89

6. Whole-Class Mini-Lessons in Selecting Texts and
    Reading Widely   91

7. Establishing Individual Conferences to Support
    Children in Selecting Texts and Reading Widely   109

8. The Question of Readability Levels   133

Part Four: Responses   147

9. Responses to Reading   149

10. Resources for Responding   169

Appendixes   195
Bibliography   225
Index   229

Foreword

Tony Stead's new book, *Good Choice! Supporting Independent Reading and Response K–6*, has come along at just the right moment for all of us who are involved in implementing classroom literacy programs. The perplexing, and sometimes vexing, issue of independent reading as an integral part of the learning day is rife with important questions:

- Will our children enjoy time alone with a book?
- Does this type of literacy event promote reading proficiency among young readers?
- Should we control the choices young readers make with texts?
- Will we level all of our books?
- Will children spend more time responding to a text than they did reading it?
- Should we expect children to read with their parents every night?

In this practical and informative book, Tony Stead leads us through each aspect of independent reading time so that we as teachers can establish a program that works for all of our children, a program that supports and nourishes the other components of our reading and writing workshops.

Tony discusses the different ways that teachers establish independent reading times—throughout the day or as part of a literacy center—but he outlines carefully his reasons for establishing a scheduled time during which children read their own choice of texts. Young learners, he says, will see this as "an important and pleasurable opportunity and take this time seriously." He also expands the function of literacy centers, a place where children can become involved in worthwhile reading and writing activities while the teacher works with a small group of students.

Teachers will find careful suggestions for implementing an independent reading program in their classrooms, beginning with procedures for borrowing books and for keeping track of who is reading what, both at home and at school. Tony's ideas for maintaining and sharing student reading logs add strength to the program. Reading logs not only promote interesting books to other children, they also make important literacy information available to the teacher: Are any of the students stuck in one genre? Are they self-selecting appropriate materials? Do their selections reveal significant facts about their literacy lives?

I especially appreciate Tony's understanding of the role parents play in building young readers, and the booklet format he provides to involve the home in meaningful ways is a valuable tool. Tony also suggests school libraries as resources that parents can use to find read-aloud materials for sharing time with their children.

A section on incorporating a variety of texts from the content areas during independent reading time changes our definition of what children could—and should—read throughout the day. By suggesting different types of texts, from nonfiction to magazines to pictures to websites, Tony opens up the discourse on literacy and moves the discussion into the new literacies research. He also validates all types of texts that children can read, especially those found on-screen (a comprehensive list of useful websites is included).

The final section of the book includes many helpful templates that teachers can use to implement wide-ranging independent reading programs. Tony's mandate—as demonstrated in all of his work—is to help teachers develop powerful and authentic literacy programs in their classrooms. He has considered every detail necessary for a worthwhile and significant independent reading time, and his suggestions will strengthen and enrich the literacy lives of children.

Reading this book is like having Tony Stead in your classroom (well, almost), in that his voice is heard clearly and always in support of the best practices we can use to develop effective literacy programs. A solid theoretical base reinforces his comprehensive knowledge of how classrooms can really work with independent reading, and his anecdotal evidence from partnerships with classroom teachers in the United States, Canada, and Australia illuminates and adds authenticity to each of his helpful suggestions.

From his engaging speeches, his practical workshops, and his thoughtful books, we know Tony as a truly professional educator. He is the consultant that teachers love to work alongside, and this new book frames perfectly his commitment to and care for teachers everywhere.

David Booth
Ontario Institute for Studies in Education
University of Toronto

Acknowledgments

I count myself fortunate to have worked with so many wonderful people who have helped me clarify and extend my thinking. My many encounters with students and educators around the world are always valued, and without them, this book would not be possible. To all, a big thank-you, and special gratitude to the following people:

The amazing teachers and administrators whom I have had the honor to work with. You have helped me explore and define best practices in the classroom. Specific thanks to the following people: Linda La Porte, Jeanette Lee, Laura Petrose, Peter Miller, Lisa Moynihan, Doreen del Santo, Helen Blackwell, John Carney, Kay Marscope, Jane Carlo, Lauren Benjamin, Julie Ramos, Paula Kingston, Mandy Carlson, Gabrielle Martinez, Melissa Perkins, Jennifer Gately, Christina Riska, Kathy King, Patty Davison, Helen Jamison, Noel Sorrento, Janet Mullins, Katie Benson, Melanie Jarrod, Linda Hadley, Laura Ramos, Katie Zerbo, Maria Santo, Franca Paduano, Judy Ballester, Michelle Gaul, and Betty Mason. Special thanks to Shane Wade, a remarkable teacher and learner. Shane, you have inspired me to better my thinking and practices. You always push me to think outside the box. To Karyn McGinley and John Sinnett, two outstanding teachers who have taken my work to new heights.

To the Twin Valley and Denton Independent School Districts, two of the finest districts in the country that have long recognized the importance of teaching reading and writing in context. Special thanks to the following people from these districts: Gina Sheehan, Jean McCarney, Judy Loeper, Alison Bond, Lee Hartman, Steph Koch, Steve Yanni, Michelle Murtaugh, Melinda Sullivan, Linda Bell, Linda Leisey, Kim Donahue, Cathy Taschner, Gail Porrazzo, Bill McKay, Sue Lloyd, Bob Pleis, Darlene Schoenly, Marcia Kellum, Tanya McGlothlin, Happy Carrico, Vicki Christenson, Sharon Betty, Kathy Morrison, Marilyn Crouse, and Darlene Jacobs. Many thanks to Karen Flavin, Adaire Wooding, and Rhonda Wilhite from the Alief Independent

School District. Thank you to Cathy Duvall from the Fort Bend Independent School District.

The incredible David Booth, whose inspirational works have had a profound effect on the thinking of so many teachers around the world, including my own. David, thank you for your encouragement and constant promotion of my work. To my friend and colleague Linda Hoyt, I so enjoy our many chats and value your friendship enormously. You are a remarkable educator. Thanks to my special friends Tomie de Paola and Bob Hetchel for their ongoing encouragement, support, and friendships. To Peggy Sherman, Beth Lothrop, Ellen Sankowski, Marsha Garelick, Joyce Jakubowski, and Mimi Aronson, who have continued to support me since I first came to the United States. Your friendships and advice are always valued.

To all my Canada friends, who show me a wonderful time whenever I visit, you always make me feel like an honorary Canadian. You're perfect ambassadors for your fine country. Specific thanks to Susan Martin O'Brien, Karen Forsyth, Wendy Graeme, Molly Falconer, Mary Saddler, Mary Macchiusi, Barry Wilson, Barb Rushton, Kathryn Brown, Ann Blackwood, Eph and Barb Bergman, Ailsa Howard, Tina Murphy, Lee-Anne Burkley, Sean Campbell, Becky Lemay, Kim Van Dongen, Brenda Thomsen, Alana Perelmutter, Joanne Clarke, Caroline Pope, Lynne Wardle-Ransom, Patrick O'Connor, Stephanie Wells, and Jolyn Mascarenhas. An extra special thank-you to Anne Brailsford, who is probably the smartest educator I know. Anne, I have learned so much from you and love our discussions. You truly push my thinking.

Accolades to the amazing and dynamic Stenhouse staff, who are always a pleasure to work with. You're a fine team. I am truly honored to be a Stenhouse author. Special thanks to Chris Downey, Jay Kilburn, and Nate Butler. An extra big thank-you to the incredible Philippa Stratton, my editor and dear friend. Working with you is such an honor. You help me define my thinking and push me to consider all possibilities.

To my dog, Snowy, who sits with me through the long hours of the night as I write. A constant and loyal companion. To my mother, Patricia, and mother-in-law, Bridge, thank you for always making me feel special. Thanks also to my nephew Jordan Smith.

And finally, to my wife, Jennifer, and to my son, Fraser, you both inspire me beyond words.

Good Choice!

PART 1

Making Time
for Independent
Reading

Establishing Independent Reading and Borrowing Routines

As a boy, I treasured independent reading time. It was a wonderful break from completing the countless exercises that filled the chalkboard, a special time of day when I could depart the world of school and enter the wonders, adventures, and remote lands awaiting me in the pages of a book. Like many people, I considered myself a self-taught reader. Although my teachers provided the necessary springboards, demonstrating how to decode and figure out word meanings, putting these techniques into practice during independent reading time proved to be the catalyst for making me a reader. The more I read on a daily basis, the more my abilities strengthened, which allowed me to connect with more complex materials. To me, reading was never a dull task. I considered it a pleasant activity that I gladly took into my home life.

Only when I became a teacher did I realize that not all of my students were like me as a child. Many of my learners were disengaged and disempowered readers. For them, reading was a chore, not a pursuit that they took into their home lives. Why was this the case? I struggled to find an answer. It was like asking, Why doesn't a child enjoy playing games or eating ice cream? It didn't seem possible that a child couldn't enjoy reading.

I asked my reluctant readers why they disliked reading. Their answers were simple yet revealing. Reading was either too difficult, hence not pleasant, or the content of their reading wasn't engaging. They hated having to do book reports on everything they read. This negative attitude was not confined to just my struggling readers; many of my more advanced readers were also disconnected because they hadn't discovered the joys in being readers and found responding to their reading a tedious task. As Mark Twain once said, "The man who does not read has no advantage over the man who cannot read."

As a young teacher, I realized that I needed to be the catalyst to connecting my learners to literature. It was no good teaching them to be readers if they were not going to be lifelong readers. First, I had to provide my learners with a focused time to read on a daily basis. I had to excite them about being readers by providing a range of reading materials based on their interests while acknowledging that these materials needed to be at reading levels they could cope with. I didn't want them to struggle through reading texts. I then needed to expand their reading repertoire so that they were not locked into reading in too narrow a field. They needed to discover the many purposes for reading and to become active participants in the selection process. I also had to consider how to assist my students as they responded to their reading—not only to get them through those dreaded test-taking situations, but also to excite them. Indeed, my task seemed more complex than I had first considered. Independent reading needed to become an integral and focused component of my daily reading program, not simply an activity for early finishers or for settling down after lunch.

When I look back on those early days as a teacher, I realize that twenty-five years later I am still faced with many of the same challenges. Many learners in our classrooms still see reading as monotonous. As teachers, we need to continuously excite all of our children about the pleasures of being readers. Over the next ten chapters, we will examine ways to make independent reading both a focused and a natural part of each day to assist all children in becoming confident, engaged readers for many purposes. We will also look at wonderful ways to help children respond to their reading in ways that make sense to them as readers.

Establishing Independent Reading Time

Within any reading program, a daily time needs be set aside for children to engage in independent reading. It is true that independent reading should occur throughout the day and for a variety of purposes, such as research; support to content understandings; rehearsing texts introduced in read-aloud, shared, and small-group instruction time; and as a springboard for writing. Indeed, Chapter 2 will examine how to ensure that independent reading occurs throughout the day; however, each day, our learners should also have time to read materials based on their own interests. For many children, this may be the only opportunity they have to read for a sustained period of time. The research to support the positive effects that self-selected independent reading has on improving children's competencies in literacy is substantial. Stephen Krashen's *The Power of Reading* cites research from around the world that shows when children are given adequate time to engage with texts on a daily basis, their improvement in literacy development is substantial. In many kindergarten through second-grade classrooms, independent reading occurs primarily as part of literacy centers. Although I support the notion that literacy centers should include independent reading, I am concerned that children are not getting ample time to read daily.

The time set aside for independent reading can vary according to grade. At the beginning of the school year, if children in a kindergarten classroom can look through literature longer than five minutes, I celebrate. But with proper scaffolds, by the year's end, these same learners are able to read and talk about literature for at least fifteen to twenty minutes daily. For children in grades two through five who are engaged in suitable texts, this time can extend beyond thirty minutes. By establishing a time for independent reading from the onset of the school year, children not only build up stamina for reading but also see it as an important and pleasurable component of their daily lives. If we teachers view reading as important, not just as a time filler, then our learners will also take this time seriously.

In the classrooms where I work, the children and I always come up with a set of guidelines to govern our independent reading time. We always involve children in coming up with rules rather than presenting them with expectations without consultation. If children are part of the decision-making process, they are more likely to accept and maintain the established code of conduct.

During Independent Reading Time You Need To:
■ Find a comfortable place to read.
■ Make sure you have enough reading material to last you for the session.

- Read quietly.
- Make sure you do not disturb others.
- Quietly select suitable texts from the classroom library if it is your day to choose.
- Raise your hand if you have a question or need something.
- Reread your material or look in the browsing boxes for more books if you finish early.
- Think about the information you are learning as your read. You may want to take some notes as you read.
- Enjoy this special time.

The K/1 Factor

In kindergarten and first-grade classrooms, establishing independent reading time at the beginning of the school year can be chaotic, especially if children come to school with limited experiences in handling books or are pre-emergent readers. It can be challenging to get these children to read beyond two minutes. It is therefore essential to provide experiences with books that will build up their reading stamina. To overcome this challenge in Linda La Porte's kindergarten classroom, we established buddy reading before independent reading. Success was ensured by pairing children we knew would work well together. We made a chart that included a photograph of each child with his or her reading buddy because many of the children would not be able to read the names of their reading buddy on the chart. We also knew that children love seeing photographs of themselves and that it would be a quick visual reference for them.

Once paired, each child was given a colored tag on a string to wear. One member of the pair had a blue tag; the other had a yellow tag. We then gave each child a book bag containing one book. The book was either one that had been read to them in a whole-class setting or a simple book with a repeated pattern and matching illustrations. It was important that children had books they were familiar with and could therefore retell, talk about using the pictures, or actually read because of the simple repetitive text. We used a lot of simple nonfiction texts to achieve this task because we knew the illustrations would promote engaged discussions. Their book bags and tags were housed in the classroom library as seen in Figure 1.1.

Linda and I demonstrated to the class what reading buddies do when they read, as seen in the following transcript:

Tony: My reading buddy is Linda, and I have the blue tag.

Figure 1.1
Children's Book Bags
and Buddy Reading
Tags

Linda: My reading buddy is Tony, and I have the yellow tag.

Tony: First, I'm going to take out my book from my book bag and tell my reading buddy the story. It doesn't matter if I can't read the words because I can tell my buddy the story using the pictures.

Linda: I'm going to make sure I listen to what Tony is saying and look at the book as he is reading it.

I then proceed to tell the story to Linda. I turn each page and either read the words or use the pictures to retell the story.

Linda: Now I'm going to take out my book and read it to Tony.

Tony: I'm going to make sure I put my book away and listen to you, Linda.

Linda then proceeds to read the book to me.

Tony: Now we're going to get some paper and write and draw about the books we read.

Linda: I'm going to draw about your book, Tony, because I liked it a lot. I'm going to draw my favorite part.

Tony: I'm going to draw and write about my favorite part of your book, Linda, and then I might draw the part I like best in my book.

Children need to see what is expected of them during the buddy reading session. The preceding transcript demonstrates the importance of showing children what the buddy reading session looks and sounds like. If another teacher is not available to act as a model for the demonstration, then using another student is equally effective.

After the demonstration, Linda and I put the pairs together and asked all the children with a blue tag to begin reading their book or to retell using the pictures. We were amazed at how they mimicked us. It was quite humorous to hear Robert using a semi-Australian accent as he retold the story to Betty. To our students, this was fun and games. I was delighted that at an early age they were already loving books. After around five minutes, we stopped the class and asked those with the blue tags to put their books away and the children with the yellow tags to take out their books and begin reading. Five minutes later we again stopped the children and handed out paper and markers for them to write about and draw their favorite parts. This task lasted another five minutes, and then we brought the session to a close.

Linda and I constructed the following chart with the children's help to outline what good buddy readers do. This chart became a useful reference for the children, and we always began our buddy reading sessions by reviewing our chart so that the children's expectations were clear.

Good Buddy Readers

Take turns reading.
Listen to each other.
Use words and pictures to tell the story.
Help each other.
Look after their books.
Write and draw about what they have read.

Each day we placed a different book in each child's book bag and repeated the routine. During this time, we circulated the room, offering support and encouragement as needed. It was not long before our learners could spend fifteen minutes each day reading and responding to the literature in their book bags. Eventually, we encouraged the children to select the books they wanted to read and respond to. Within three months, we were able to move from buddy reading toward independent reading that included children writing and drawing about their own selections. Instituting a firm structure at the beginning of the school year, coupled with providing appropriate scaffolds, had helped our learners transition into an independent reading routine for at least fifteen minutes daily.

A useful reference for setting up buddy reading is the book *Buddy Reading: Cross-Age Tutoring in a Multiage School*, by Gail Whang, Katharine Davies Samway, and Mary Pippitt (1995).

Setting Up Borrowing Routines

A common problem in most classrooms is borrowing time. When children are asked to borrow from the classroom library, often a stampede occurs, resulting in children fighting over books, accompanied by unacceptable noise levels. It can take up to fifteen minutes for students to find a book, and when we consider that most of them are just grabbing any book regardless of the text's difficulty, it becomes evident that this is ineffective and a waste of time. Thirty children in a classroom library at once is not wise!

One way to eliminate confusion is to allow children to borrow a certain number of books for the week on a rotational basis. In Jeanette Lee's first-grade classroom where I worked, each child had a book bag with his or her name on it. The book bags were placed in baskets in the classroom. Each day during independent reading time, six children browsed through the classroom library and selected books for the week. In this way, by the end of the week, all thirty children had borrowed books. Initially, Jeanette and I set aside one day so that all the children could borrow books for the week. That way everyone started off with books to engage with during independent reading time.

Jeanette placed each child's name on a chart so that the student knew which day to borrow. See Figure 1.2, and refer to Appendix A for a graphic organizer you may wish to use. We used Velcro to attach students' names to the chart. If any students were absent, we could remove their name tags and put them aside to signify that these students needed borrowing time when they returned to class. Velcro also enabled us to reorganize the chart should we wish to have specific groups of students borrowing on a particular day. For example, if a group of students encountered difficulties selecting appropriate material, they were grouped together so that we could provide additional assistance.

At first, the children wanted to borrow twenty or more books at a time, so we held a whole-class discussion and decided that they would borrow five or six books for the week. In addition, browsing tubs were

Monday	Tuesday	Wednesday	Thursday	Friday
Julie	Peter	Lucy	Sara	Jennifer
Marcus	George	Maverick	Cathy	Alexis
Jose	Fred	Jason	Tina	Carla
Ellen	Elana	Daniel	Mary M.	Paul
Mary T.	Betty	Mary C.	Tatiana	Juan
Cynthia	Maria	Robert	Mike	Kate

Figure 1.2
Book Changing
Schedule

placed on each table so that if children finished with their selections during independent reading time, they could borrow other materials to read from the tubs at their tables. I found that Jeanette's routine was equally effective with kindergarten children.

Laura Petrose, a second-grade teacher from Queens, New York, had her children select books for the week as a literacy center activity while she conducted small-group instruction. Laura also had an organizational board so that children knew when it was their day to borrow. Although this worked effectively for Laura, she commented that she incorporated the book borrowing as a literacy center activity only when children knew how to make wise selections. She knew that initially sending children to borrow books while she conducted guided reading would be ineffective as she needed to be available to give support.

I know many teachers of grades three through five who don't have a scheduled borrowing time. In Peter Miller's grade five class, we found that the children were able to borrow materials as needed throughout the week. These learners were engaged readers, with many years of experience borrowing appropriate texts. By fifth grade, many of our learners were reading novels and lengthy pieces of nonfiction and only needed to borrow every other week. If Peter and I discovered that specific children were having difficulties borrowing, then we gave support during independent conferences. See Chapter 7 for more details.

Record-Keeping

Record-keeping in the form of reading logs is an important part of independent reading because they serve many purposes:

- They allow the teacher to track the types of materials children are reading, thus enabling the teacher to broaden children's reading repertoire.
- They allow the children to see what they are reading and give them a sense of success.
- They enable children to share their selections and to give recommendations to their peers.
- They enable parents to see and celebrate what their children are reading.

Once children are able to record their selections in a timely fashion, they can maintain their own reading logs. This usually occurs sometime between second and third grades. Children can log their selections in many ways, and I've used many different examples over the years. I am currently using a log based on work I did in Lisa Moynihan's third-grade classroom. See Figure 1.3, and refer to Appendix B for a sample.

Apart from keeping track of reading selections, this log allows children to reflect on the specific types of fiction and nonfiction they are reading. When children become fluent readers, they often read in a narrow field. This is especially true for their fiction selections. They find a favorite author and read every book by that person. I remember after my son read *Brian's Winter*, he read every book that Gary Paulsen had written. This is natural not just for children but also adults. I know that, after I have read a great book, I automatically look for other publications by that author. However, children can become trapped in reading only books by a specific author or in a specific genre. For example, once my fourth-grade boys discovered mysteries and science fiction, their reading was dominated by these two genres. Thus, recording the text types of their selections onto their logs enables me to suggest how they can extend their reading repertoire.

Figure 1.3
A Page from Amanda's Reading Log

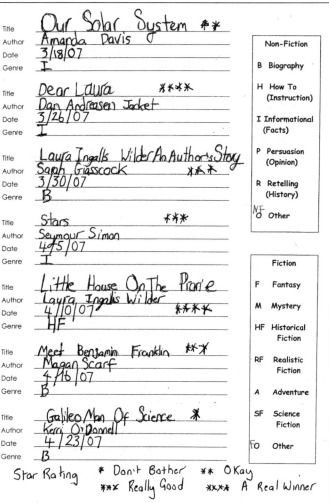

Sharing Reading Logs

Reading logs are also a wonderful tool for students to use when making recommendations to their peers. Amanda's log (Figure 1.3) includes a star rating at the bottom of each page that allows her to remember what she thought of each selection and give advice to other children who are looking for something to read. In my own classroom, I ensured that at least once a month my students looked at each other's logs and wrote down titles of material they planned to read in the future based on the recommendations of their peers. My students recorded these as seen in Figure 1.4. Refer to Appendix C for a sample.

My students loved recommending particular texts to each other. I remember that Jason, who at the time was reading *Bridge to Terabithia*, put the book down after three chapters and told me he didn't like it and thought it deserved a one-star rating. He said he was giving the book to Katherine because he thought she would love it because it was her kind of book. It was terrific to see that a community of readers was being established and that my learners were as interested in their peers' reading as they were in their own.

Figure 1.4

Daniel's Log of Books and Magazines He Wants to Read

Books and Magazines I Want to Read

Name Daniel   Grade 5

Name of book/magazine	Author	Recommended by
A Single Shard	Linda Sue Park	James
Killer Whales	Sandra Markle	Patrick
The Prince of Tarn	Hazel Hutchins	Helena
Matilda	Roald Dahl	Katherine
David Beckham Soccer Superstar	Grey Roza	Jose
Holes	Louis Sacher	Maria
Real life Magazine Places around the world	Rosen	Marcus
The History of baseball	Helmer and Owens	Michael T.

Reading Logs for Children (K–2)

Although reading logs serve many purposes, it is not feasible to expect young children to record their selections onto a log. Indeed, in kindergarten classrooms, this could take the children all day. Likewise, it is unrealistic to expect the classroom teacher to keep track of every piece of literature each child reads. Usually, by first grade, children can be reading a book a day, which means the classroom teacher could be recording up to twenty-eight selections daily. This is not the best use of a teacher's time.

When I worked with Doreen del Santo in her first-grade classroom, we decided that every Friday we would ask the students to tell us their favorite selection for the week and record this onto their log. See Figure 1.5, and refer to Appendix D for a reading log you may wish to use. In

Name Yolanda Martinez	**Grade** One		
Title In Went Goldilocks (F)	Date 9/7	Level C	
Title Kitten Chased a Fly (F)	Date 9/14	Level C	
Title Fast Machines (N)	Date 9/21	Level D	
Title Catch That Frog (F)	Date 9/28	Level E	
Title Shadows (N)	Date 10/5	Level D	
Title Animal Babies (N)	Date 10/12	Level E	
Title The Baby (F)	Date 10/19	Level E	
Title Cookie's Week (F)	Date 10/26	Level F	
Title The Gingerbread Man (F)	Date 11/2	Level F	
Title Snails (N)	Date 11/9	Level F	
Title Smarty Pants (F)	Date 11/16	Level E	
Title Grandpa's Cookies (F)	Date 11/23	Level F	
Title Animals at the Zoo (N)	Date 11/30	Level F	
Title Dragonflies (N)	Date 12/7	Level G	
Title Carla's Ribbons (F)	Date 12/14	Level G	
Title Whales (N)	Date 12/20	Level G	

Key : N–Nonfiction   F– Fiction

Figure 1.5
A Page from Yolanda's Reading Log

this way, we kept more of a global track of the literature children were reading without having to record every selection. We had been having conversations with the children about the importance of reading both fiction and nonfiction and decided it was important to include this information on the log. It indicated whether they were reading widely and including informational texts in their weekly reading. At times, we asked them about their favorite nonfiction piece for the week to ensure that the log was reflecting their nonfiction selections.

Whether to include the reading level of the book based on the Fountas and Pinnell leveling system was an issue we considered closely. The disadvantage of including a level was that children could become locked into selecting only books with higher levels to impress both their peers and their parents. This could lead to their selecting texts that were too difficult for them to read. This would, in turn, negate the primary reason for independent reading: to enable children to enjoy books they could actually read. To alleviate this possible dilemma, we knew it would be important to have conversations with the children about the importance of selecting suitable or just-right texts for independent reading. We further realized we would have to support them with their selections. Chapters 6 and 7 will discuss this in detail.

The advantage of keeping levels was obvious. It would allow us to track children's selections to ensure they were choosing appropriate texts. Doreen and I noticed that many children were struggling when it came to selecting suitable texts, so including the level was beneficial as a monitoring strategy. The levels gave us a quick visual of how children were progressing on the literacy continuum. As seen in Yolanda's log, she is now comfortable selecting texts at a level G, which indicates a growth from the beginning of the school year. Although we eventually decided to track the levels, this choice needs to be made by each teacher. Usually, by the time children become fluent readers and are able to self-select appropriate materials, recording the levels of their selections onto their logs is no longer necessary.

Home Reading

Bernice Cullinan from New York University collated significant quantitative and qualitative research that showed a strong link between home reading and proficiency in literacy (Long and Henderson 1973; Greaney 1980; Hepler and Hickman 1982; Reutzel and Hollingsworth 1991; Shapiro and White 1991; Barbieri 1995; Short 1995). In their report *Reading for Change*, the Organization for Economic Co-operation and Development (2002) showed a generally a higher level of reading profi-

Percentile Rank	Minutes per Day Reading Outside of School	Words Encounters per Year
98th	67.3	4,733,000
90th	33.4	2,357,000
70th	16.9	1,168,000
50th	9.2	601,000
30th	4.3	251,000
10th	1.0	51,000
2nd	0.0	0

Figure 1.6
Growth in Reading and How Children Spend Their Time Outside of School (Adapted from Anderson, Wilson, and Fielding 1988)

ciency in students who read in their free time. Furthermore, they found that students from disadvantaged backgrounds who read at home outperformed students from middle- and upper-class backgrounds who didn't read at home. This report would appear to support research by Anderson, Wilson, and Fielding (1988), who found that children who spend substantial time reading at home rank as the strongest readers. See Figure 1.6. Although this research holds no surprises, it does highlight the importance of home reading. Whereas a focused school reading program will help our learners become better readers, those children who take reading into their lives outside the classroom become our strongest readers. However, we cannot assume that because we send books home with our children each night they are being read.

For many years, I diligently ensured that my students took books home each night and even had parents sign their children's take home logs to verify that their children had read the material. I didn't consider that in many cases children were telling their parents they had read their take home selections and the parents were signing the forms regardless of whether this was the case. This didn't dawn on me until I became a parent. One morning when my son was in second grade, he told me that I had to sign his take home log or else he would be in trouble. It was 7:30 and I was already running late, so I simply signed the form in the hope that he had actually read his selections. He was an avid reader and most nights I spent time with him reading. I didn't think much of it then; however, later, my feelings of guilt set in. If I as a teacher and educator was engaging in this practice, then how many other parents were doing likewise but on a daily basis? And what about the children who were not avid readers? Did their parents also sign their forms in the hope that their children had read their selections? How many parents actually took time to monitor their children's reading at home, especially if there were other children to care for or the parents worked long hours? Were my expectations unrealistic?

I soon realized that simply sending a log home for parents to sign was not enough. I had to go one step further and help them realize the importance of home reading. I also had to acknowledge that this might not be a nightly occurrence. I further realized that I couldn't rely only on the parents. I had to ensure that my students wanted to take reading into their home lives so that, even if their parents were too busy to spend time with them each night monitoring their reading, I could still be certain they were engaging with literature.

Educating Parents on the Importance of Home Reading

Most parents want to help their children as readers, but many don't know how. For these parents, the ritual of hearing their child read each night becomes more of a task than a pleasure. Without guidance, many parents use this time to quiz their children on the number of words they can pronounce or their reading level. The joy of spending time with their children over a book is lost. Furthermore, when children reach grade three and are deemed fluent readers, some parents take little to no interest in their children's home reading. When I asked one parent why she didn't bother to monitor her son's reading, she answered, "But he can read; what's the point?"

I have found that education is the key to helping parents assist their children with home reading. I would always organize an information evening for parents on how best to help their children at home, but sadly, not all the parents would attend. I found that one of the best methods to help educate parents was to give them an informational brochure at parent/teacher conferences. I am reluctant to give these out to the children to take home because I can't always guarantee they will make it into the hands of their parents. Unless I personally gave the brochure to parents and impressed on them the importance of home reading, the brochure became yet another form that went home without being given high priority. These brochures need to be simple and informative. They need to demonstrate step by step not only how parents can help their children but also why it is important to take an active interest in their children's home reading regardless of their children's ages.

These brochures should be translated into different languages so that all parents regardless of their English proficiency are able to engage with home reading with their children. This is an important consideration, especially for bilingual and English as a second language learners (ESLs). Parents need to know that reading to and with their children in the home language is not just acceptable but desirable. If children are to transition into proficiency in English, they need a strong base in their home language. Refer to Appendix E for a sample of a brochure that can be sent home for children in kindergarten through second grade. Appendix F has a brochure suitable for parents of children in grades three through five. Note: Copy the two pages from each appendix back to back then fold to make a brochure.

Another way to assist parents is to set up a lending library in the classroom. See Figure 1.7. I got this wonderful idea many years ago from a group of librarians I had worked with in New York who had established these in the school library. By gathering good books from both my classroom library and the school library, I was able to suggest great books for parents to read to or with their children.

Encouraging Children to Read at Home

Ultimately, the child has to want to become a reader regardless of whether their parents take an active interest in their home reading. Children will only freely engage in an activity if they see an identifiable purpose or derive pleasure from that pursuit. And reading *is* fun, so it should not be difficult for teachers to promote home reading as a pleasurable pursuit, not a task that has to be completed.

Figure 1.7
Parents' Lending Library

In John Carney's first-grade classroom, we achieved this by first discussing with the children the kinds of books they liked to read at home. The children enjoyed this conversation, but when we asked them where they like to read, our conversations became interesting.

I told the children that, when I was in first grade, I loved to make a tent under my sheets and use a flashlight to read at night. I loved having all the lights off and reading underneath the sheets in my own little world. I did this because my parents made me turn off my bedroom light by 9 p.m., and I wanted to stay up and read. I loved trying to read at least two of my books without being caught. The children were fascinated by this story. It was as if reading had suddenly become a dangerous and highly desirable game. "Did you ever get caught?" asked Harold. "Once," I replied. "What happened?" asked the children. "My mom told me that if I got caught again, I would be fed to dinosaurs." The children laughed, and I could see that this game of reading at home had suddenly become more interesting. Together, we made a list of the places we like to read at home.

Where We Like to Read at Night
Underneath the bed covers with a flashlight
In a comfy chair
Under the bed
On a big rug
At my desk
In front of the fire when it's cold
Next to the air conditioner when it's hot
In bed
Stretched out on a couch
Outside in the garden
In the park
To my mom and dad in the lounge room
At the kitchen table

The next morning the children came in excited and eager to talk about where they had read the night before. Many said that they had changed locations and tried a different reading place. Naturally, many had tried out reading underneath the bedcovers with a flashlight. I told the children I, too, had changed my reading spot. They were excited. Home reading was suddenly like belonging to an important club. I was reminded of Frank Smith's book *Joining the Literacy Club*. It is important for children to want to become members of that club.

Although John and I were pleased with the children's enthusiasm, we still needed to maintain the momentum. We needed to make certain that the children were engaging not only with literature they loved but also had material at suitable readability levels. Ultimately, where they read was irrelevant; that they were reading was what was critical. We conferred with each child once a week to monitor both their school and home reading. Only by taking an active interest in each child as a reader could we maintain their wonderful enthusiasm. Refer to Chapter 7 for information about setting up and maintaining individual conferences.

In Helen Blackwell's fifth grade, motivating her children to read at night was not so simple. If children are disconnected from reading by the time they reach third grade, then reconnecting them is an uphill battle, which was certainly the case with Helen's children. With the exception of a handful of learners, her children really disliked reading. This was because these children in past years had been given little choice in selecting reading materials. Books were assigned to them, and lengthy book reports had to be completed. Helen and I set up borrowing routines and established conversations about literature. We encouraged our learners to discuss what they liked to read and included comics, magazines, newspapers, and the computer as choices. We abandoned book reports and gave children choices in selecting materials. With the assistance of our students, we established a comprehensive classroom library that became the heartbeat of the classroom. (Refer to Chapters 3 and 4 for further information.) As in John's first-grade class, individual conferences were established to not only monitor children's selections but also to demonstrate that we were interested in them as readers. The excitement generated in the classroom soon spilled over into their home reading. Before long, we were confident that our children were reading not just because it was expected but because it was recreational.

Keeping Track of Take Home Books

For many years in my own classroom, children would borrow up to five books each night, and I would attempt to keep track of these selections in a notebook. The next morning I would diligently check to see whether each book had been brought back so that I could record its return. This proved to be a time-consuming daily ritual. When I reflected on what happened to this notebook at the end of the year, I realized I had thrown it away. A more effective method was to allow the children to take home just one or two books each night and for them to record the titles in a notebook. This saved me at least twenty minutes each day. The teacher's decision about how many books go home each night depends on many factors. In fourth or fifth grade, for instance, when children are reading novels or longer pieces of nonfiction, one piece per night is ample. With younger children who are reading shorter books, more than one may be warranted.

The K/1 Factor

In Kay Marscope's kindergarten classroom, having children record their take home books was not feasible because most of the children were unable to do so and the time taken to complete such a task was extensive. Kay and I bought pockets with matching cards similar to those used by librarians. Parent aides helped us glue pockets into the back of

Figure 1.8
Take Home Chart

the books. The title of the book was recorded on the accompanying pull-out card. Kay and I then wrote the name of each child on a pocket and placed these pockets on a chart. The children would then take the pull-out card from the book they wished to borrow and place it into the pocket bearing their name on the chart. The following morning, the children brought back their take home book and placed the pull-out card from the chart back into the pocket of the book. In this way, each morning Kay and I were able to see which children had brought back their take home selections. See Figure 1.8.

The Sister Mary Effect

Sister Mary, the principal at my wife's former school, didn't believe that keeping track of homebound books was a priority. The school was in a low socioeconomic area in Melbourne, Australia, and many of the parents were unable to read. Most of the students were on free and reduced lunch. Sister Mary was a pioneer in trying to ensure that literacy was a priority at the school and in the home; therefore, each year, she would allocate a certain percentage of money within her budget to replace books that weren't returned from home. When I questioned why more attempts were not made to recover books, her answer was enlightening. She replied, "If our children are not returning books then our literacy program must be working. If we are getting books into the home then we are on the way to achieving our goals. If they see books as valuable enough to steal then we are producing lifelong readers."

Independent Reading
Throughout the Day

In addition to having an identified time to read materials they have personally selected as outlined in Chapter 1, students need to have other reading opportunities throughout the day. These are teacher-directed, or teacher-initiated, encounters. Wherein self-choice selections place the responsibility on the child for selecting and engaging with texts based on interests, teacher-directed selections seek to strengthen children's reading competencies through specific reading encounters established by the teacher. These encounters give children the opportunity to practice and master independently skills taught in whole-class and small-group encounters. These contexts may include literacy or work stations; author studies; rereading known texts used in read-aloud, shared reading, and guided reading situations; and content studies. Book clubs and literature circles are also

23

opportunities for children to engage in concentrated independent encounters with books and are discussed in detail in Chapter 9.

These assigned reading encounters, although critical to developing reading skills and strategies, should never be used to replace independent reading time when children are making their own selections. Rather they should be an additional component to a balanced reading program. By fifth and sixth grades, teacher-directed focuses can dominate children's independent reading, and the joy of picking up a book or magazine for pleasure can be lost. The demands on our learners to read for content understandings in science and social studies, together with reading for test-taking situations and responding to teacher-selected literature, can give our students little time to pick up literature and read for pure pleasure. Consequently, children can soon view reading negatively. These teacher-directed or teacher-initiated reading encounters should be presented so that children can derive pleasure from reading in the same way they do when they are self-selecting materials.

The News/Bulletin Board

Creating a news board is an excellent way of keeping children informed of upcoming events both within the school and in their communities. In my classroom, I divided the notice board into different sections with such titles as "school news," "local news," "international news," "weather," "sports results," "lost and found," "good movies to see," "great books to read," and "field trips." The children were encouraged to bring in articles from newspapers to pin under the relevant sections of the board and to write pieces and post them in the relevant category. At the end of each week, an appointed monitor would take down old news to make way for new entries.

As part of the news board, I also had what I called Person of the Week. Each week I selected a child to write about him- or herself. For children who found this task difficult, I gave them an organizer to keep track of biographical details. The organizer dealt with items such as where they were born, their dislikes, and their favorite color, toy, book, and foods. An example of this organizer can be found in Appendix G. The selected child would then place a picture of him- or herself next to the biographical details and pin this onto the news board for other children to read throughout the week. The Person of the Week was a coveted position within the classroom. The position had special privileges, such as being the first to be dismissed each day and being the teacher's messenger. My goal was to ensure that every child in my classroom received the honor. This was particularly beneficial for children who found it difficult to stay on task. It gave them the incentive to improve so that they could receive the special honor. It was amazing to see how excited my students became when a new person of the week placed his or her biographical details on the news board. I found it necessary to have a roster system, since all the children wanted to read about the new person as soon as the information went onto the news board.

Independent Reading as Part of Literacy Stations and Centers

Over the past ten years, emphasis on establishing literacy work stations (Diller 2003, 2005) or literacy centers has grown. These literacy stations and centers have become a huge focus in classrooms, especially in the early elementary years. They establish a management structure that seeks to strengthen children's literacy development while enabling the teacher to conduct small-group instruction. The essential ingredients in making these stations and centers work effectively have been well documented by educators. In *The Literacy Center* (1997), Lesley Mandel Morrow gives wonderful insights into the effective ingredients of a literacy center as do Dorn, French, and Jones (1998) in *Apprenticeship in Literacy*. Debbie Diller's *Literacy Work Stations* (2003) and *Practice with Purpose* (2005) teem with great ideas for establishing, maintaining, and monitoring literacy stations at both primary and intermediate levels.

Although these stations and centers can be a wonderful way to strengthen children's aptitudes as readers, we must make sure children are actually reading at some of these centers and not engaged in activities that keep them busy while the teacher conducts small-group instruction. Over the past ten years, I have found that the latter is the case. For many years, in my own classroom, it was questionable how much reading was actually occurring during center time. Although I had put much effort into establishing wonderful routines and activities for children to engage in while I conducted small-group instruction, I had given little thought to the amount of time they were actually reading. As an experiment, I randomly selected five children and monitored how much reading they were doing at the centers. Selecting a different child each day and using a stopwatch, I timed these five children over the course of a week. I did likewise the next week with five different children. I was stunned to find that on average, each child spent 5.4 minutes during a 40-minute session actually reading. The children spent most of their time talking, moving around the room, going to the bathroom, drawing, writing, and playing with alphabet and word cards. Although these activities are valuable, I realized they were occurring during the reading block. My children were doing everything but reading.

I made changes to ensure that reading was the core of each center. In some instances, I eliminated centers that were not giving my students an opportunity to engage in some form of reading. A sample of some of the literacy centers I have used to encourage children to read independently follows. To ensure success, show children how each center operates through multiple and ongoing teacher demonstrations. Next to each center I have included the approximate grade areas for which centers are appropriate.

Big Book Center (K–3)

In the Big Book center, children reread Big Books and charts that have been introduced to the class during shared reading encounters. With this center, you can have up to six children gathered around the Big Book bookstand or easel. One child is the teacher and uses a pointer to point to the words while the other children are seated on the floor and join in with the reading.

Considerations for Success
The texts should be books and charts that all children have heard before so that everyone can join in with the reading. Children will need to keep their voices low as they read so that other learners are not disturbed. Children will need to know the order in which they will be responsible for playing the teacher.

Overhead Center (3–6)

In the overhead center, children use overhead transparencies from classroom shared reading encounters to reread materials and discuss them with fellow group members. The children can decide whether they read the text together, take turns reading specific sections of the text, or read independently before they embark on a discussion. These discussions could center on whole-class comprehension focuses such as inferring, connecting, summarizing, evaluating, and point of view.

Considerations for Success
The overhead projector and screen will need to be set up in an area that will not distract the other children. The overhead transparencies should be ones already introduced to the class in whole-class settings. The children will need to know their focus for discussions about the

text before the reading. This should be made clear before the children go to the center.

Reading the Room Center (K–3)

In this center, children can work with a partner to reread print that is displayed around the room, that is, poems, charts, maps, strategy charts, word lists, names, information on the news board, and so on. Give the children a pointer to use as they are reading the different texts displayed in the room.

Another alternative is a word search in which children are asked to search the room for specific information: How many times can you find your name written? How many words can you find with d at the end? Find as many words as you can with the rime "ail." Look for the high-frequency word *when*, and record how many times you can find it. The word searches should correspond with vocabulary and word lessons previously introduced during whole-class discussions.

Examples of Read Around the Room Searches
- How many times can you find your name written?
- How many questions can you find?
- How many words end with *ed, s,* and *t*?
- How many words with the *k* sound?
- How many words with the spelling pattern _____?
- How many times can you find the word _____?
- How many words can you find that begin with a capital letter?

Considerations for Success
This can be a noisy activity, because children get excited when they find words that they are looking for. It is advisable to have children work in pairs and restrict the number of pairs engaged in this activity at one time. Encourage children to use pointers to read with and to say words in a whisper.

Buddy or Partner Reading Center (K–6)

In buddy reading, children work with a partner to read and talk about texts read together. Children can take turns to read a page or a section. After finishing the reading, children should discuss what they have read.

The selected texts should be those encountered in read-aloud, shared reading, guided reading, or materials self-selected by the children.

Considerations for Success

You will need to pair children who work well together and are able to read the text. For pre-emergent and beginning readers, use texts that have already been introduced to the class so that they know the story and can read it from memory. Children will need to know the focus of their discussions after reading the text. You will need to make this focus clear before they begin buddy reading.

Poems, Chants, Songs, and Rhymes Center (K–6)

In this center, you will need copies of poems, chants, songs, and rhymes that have been introduced to the class during read-aloud and shared reading encounters. Mount these onto oak tag and either laminate them or put them into plastic pockets. These can be housed in a basket titled "Poems, Songs, Rhymes, and Chants." Alternatively, place them in plastic pockets and put them into a binder. Children can select pieces to practice reciting either individually or in pairs. Poems children have written themselves can be added to the binder so it becomes a growing collection.

When I taught second grade, my students tape-recorded their favorite poems, rhymes, and chants at this center. I provided copies of the poems, rhymes, and chants so that the children could read along as they listened to the tape. I found this was particularly beneficial for my English as a second language learners.

Reading Favorite Read-Alouds Center (K–6)

In this center, children select favorite read-aloud texts to reread individually or in pairs. These could be housed in a basket or container with the label "Our Favorite Read-Alouds." After the teacher reads a new read-aloud, children can vote to decide whether they think it is good enough to be housed in the favorite read-aloud basket. Alternatively, each week you could have two children select a new read-aloud to add to the basket and another two children decide on a read-aloud that will be removed from the basket. This will ensure the basket never becomes too full and changes every week.

The Science Center (K–6)

Children are encouraged to read and to explore information they are learning from reading informational texts and observing specific objects from nature. Books, together with pictures, magnifying glasses, and specific objects, animals, and plants, can be placed at this center.

Encourage children to bring in interesting objects for the science table such as shells, bones, and rocks.

After you have modeled how to use the science center, create a chart that tells children what to do at the center.

At the Science Table You Need to:

1. Choose a book from the basket that may interest you.
2. Read your book for at least ten minutes.
3. Close your book and think about what you have read.
4. Look at objects at the center that are about what you are reading to compare them with what you have read.
5. Talk to other people at the center to see what information they are discovering.
6. Make notes about what you learned in the class notebook. You may include drawings.
7. Check your information with what you read.
8. Share your findings with another group member.

Children can record their observations into a class notebook that is kept at the center. For pre-emergent and early readers in kindergarten and grade one, simple observations can be made from the pictures in books together with the objects. The children could write and draw about what they are discovering on an individual observation sheet, as seen in Figure 2.1. Kian has looked at the pictures from a book about ants and observed the ant farm to record and illustrate his observations.

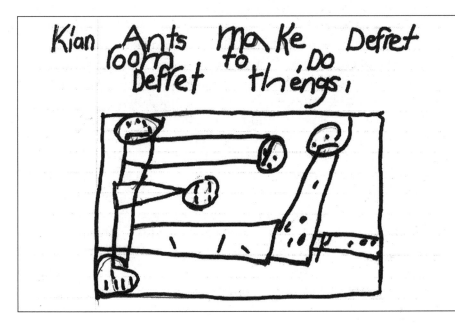

Figure 2.1
Kian's Observations About Ants

Considerations for Success

The purpose of this center is to get children to actively read and to compare what they are reading with what they are observing. Have matching literature for the objects that are placed on the science table. If no published texts are available, then information printed from the Internet can be used.

Listening Center (K–6)

In the listening center, children read along with familiar taped stories, songs, poems, and texts used in read-aloud, shared, and guided reading sessions. You will need multiple copies of the text to distribute to each child.

Considerations for Success

This center depends on the equipment working effectively, so it is advisable to check this out before sending children to the center. Many books are now on CDs, so having children gathered around a small CD player is a good option. If the volume is low, then the noise does not interfere with the learning of the other children, especially if the CD player is positioned in a corner. Not wearing earphones is an added bonus because many times they do not work or they get tangled. In one classroom where I worked, the teacher had individual Walkmans for the children to listen to.

Matching and Sequencing (K–2)

In this center, children can reconstruct texts that have been introduced in shared or guided reading encounters. For each book in this center, write the text from the book onto individual sentence strips so that the children can sequence them using the book as a guide. Use a large pocket chart and sentence strips so children can work together. Alternatively, you could have the text from the book photocopied onto a sheet of paper in random order so that each child has to cut out each sentence or group of sentences and paste them down onto another sheet of paper in the correct order. Then they use the book and read their sentences to ensure they're pasted down in sequential order. Another idea is to have the children cut out the individual sentences or groups of sentences, attach them to separate pieces of paper, and staple the pages together. The children can add their own illustrations to make their own take home book.

Consideration for Success

This activity takes time to organize, especially if the children are going to cut out sentences and paste them down. Materials will need to be readily available. Children should read the book before beginning this activity and then read their sentences before reconstructing the text. After reconstructing their text, they should read the sentences using the book as a guide. The focus of this activity is sequencing events; therefore, multiple readings are important. This is not a simple matching activity. This center requires ongoing whole-class demonstrations.

Independent Reading and Author Studies

Specific author studies are a valuable means of strengthening students' understandings of plot, setting, recurring themes, connections, and literary devices such as mood, voice, and author craft.

As a classroom teacher, each year I would select a specific author and provide my children with copies of the author's books to explore. The author study would take from one to three weeks, and we would spend between twenty and thirty minutes daily studying the works of that author. The authors I chose depended on the suitability of their materials, which was based on the interests and the reading levels of my children. For instance, an author study on Eric Carle was terrific for first graders because most children were able to read his books independently, and many of his books were about animals and insects, which are of high interest to first-grade children. Note: Author studies can be on books that children cannot read independently. In this scenario, the teacher can read the author's books to the children, which will provide the springboard for discussions.

First, I collect as many copies of the author's publications as possible. In addition to publications I already own, I also collected books from the school library and my local public library. When implementing an author study be sure to have enough books for each child to have access to his or her own book. If this is not possible, then two children can share one book and the children can buddy read. An assortment of the author's publications are best, rather than having twenty-seven copies of the same book, because I want my children to look for recurring themes and author craft. After I have amassed enough books, I place them into several baskets and label the baskets with the author's name.

I begin the study by reading one of the books to the class to immerse them in the author's works and promote discussions. After the reading, the children can talk about the book based on discussion areas I provide. I place these headings on a chart and record children's observations, as seen in Figure 2.2.

Over the next few weeks, the children read different books by the selected author, either individually or in pairs. At the end of each

Author Study: Tomie de Paola

About Tomie
- Born in Connecticut in 1934.
- Published over 200 books.
- He owns a dog.
- He lives in New Hampshire.
- His Godson is Fraser Stead.
- He always loved to draw.

Messages in His Stories
- Be proud of yourself
- Try your best.
- Be good to others.
- Never tell lies.

Author Craft
- Uses humor to tell stories and give messages.
- Has naughty characters that we like.
- Gives us lots of details
- Makes us think about our lives.
- Different settings

His Pictures
- He uses lots of folk art.
- He paints his pictures.
- He paints lots of doves in his pictures.
- Great colors.

What We Like
- The way he tells his stories.
- Has books about the same characters. You get to really know them.
- Writes about different things.
- His folktales.

Our Connections
- Oliver Button because he does what interests him.
- Strega Nona because we have relatives like her.
- Big Anthony because we all do stupid things. He makes us laugh at ourselves.
- Other folktales
- Some of the characters remind us of our friends and family
- Nana Upstairs Nana Downstairs - We think about our grandmas getting old.

Figure 2.2
Author Study on Tomie de Paola

session, I bring the children together to discuss what they have discovered and add their findings to the chart. For the section titled "About the Author," the biographical details in the books, together with researching websites about the selected author, provide the children with a wealth of information. It is also useful to write a class letter to the author and send this to the author's publisher. I tell the children that the author may not reply because he or she is busy writing or illustrating new books, but we usually receive a letter from the publisher. Most well-known authors have someone to handle letters from children; sometimes a signed letter from the author will arrive. The children are thrilled when this occurs.

This chart acts as a great springboard for children to examine their own story writing and the craft they are using to hook their readers. I also encourage children to conduct their own author studies of their favorite authors and give them an organizer to assist them with the task. Refer to Appendix H for a copy.

Discussion categories can vary and will differ depending on the grade area taught. I found that when conducting author studies with children in upper elementary school grades, the categories became more specific about the author's craft and included mood, voice, use of suspense, recurring themes, character traits, and emotions the author evoked. For children in lower elementary school grades, the categories were simple and dealt primarily with likes, dislikes, reactions, and connections.

Independent Reading and Content Studies

An important function of independent reading is it gives students the opportunity to gain knowledge about topics explored in science and social studies units. Setting up a time for students to gather information from books, from magazines, or from the computer should be an integral component of content teaching. Sadly, in some third- through sixth-grade classrooms, children are presented with a science or social studies textbook as the core method for obtaining content knowledge. Gaining content knowledge should be an active and interactive process of inquiry. Students need to know how to look through many texts to gain content information, rather than relying on one set source. They need to become what Chaille and Britain (2003) term *theory builders*—students who think, question, share, and experiment with ideas, rather than passive receivers of information from one set source.

One way to encourage inquiry-based learning is to set up research stations with reading materials directly linked to content topics. For example, in Jane Carlo's fourth-grade classroom in Texas, students were exploring space as part of a science unit. Jane set up six baskets with texts about space that included books, small charts, pictures, and information from the Internet and magazines. For teachers who do have prescribed science or social studies texts, copies of these can be incorporated into the baskets. Jane established six baskets so that each table had access to reading materials throughout the unit of study.

These baskets were readily available for children to browse through as they explored the unit and were the major tool for helping them obtain content knowledge based on the science curriculum. For example, when Jane wanted the children to find out about a specific planet, she gave them an organizer, as seen in Figure 2.3. Refer to Appendix I for an organizer you may wish to use. She then suggested they use the

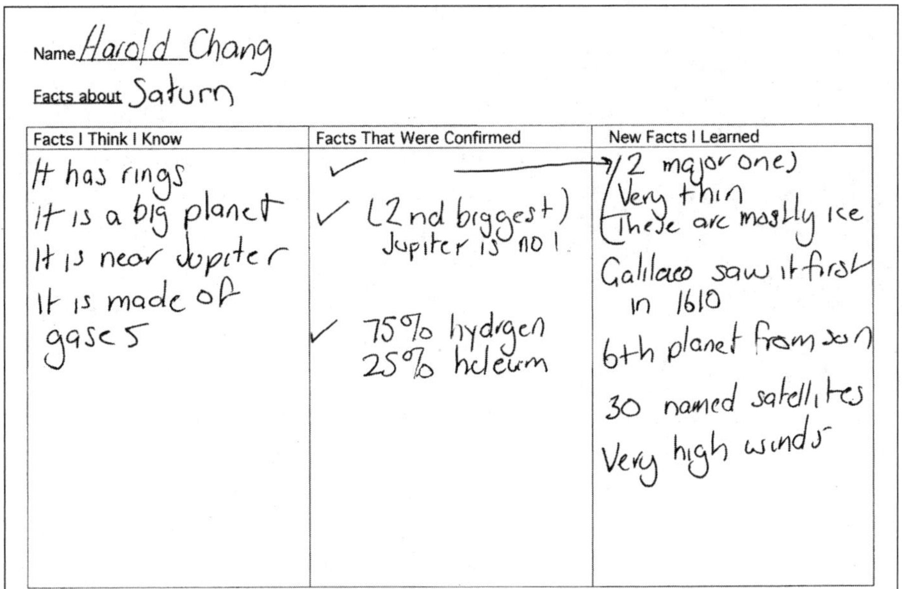
Name Harold Chang

Facts about Saturn

Facts I Think I Know	Facts That Were Confirmed	New Facts I Learned
It has rings	✓ →	2 major ones) Very thin (These are mostly ice
It is a big planet	✓ (2nd biggest) Jupiter is no 1.	
It is near Jupiter		Galilaeo saw it first in 1610
It is made of gases	✓ 75% hydrgen 25% heleum	6th planet from sun
		30 named satellites
		Very high winds

Figure 2.3
Harold's Organizer for Saturn

materials in the baskets to see what they could find out about the planet. Jane first asked the children to record what they thought they knew about the planet so that when they looked through the materials in the basket, they were actively reading not only to gain new insights but also to confirm prior thinking. This organizer was based on a strategy called the Reading and Analyzing Nonfiction Strategy (RAN) and is discussed in more detail in Chapter 5. A detailed account on using the RAN effectively can also be found in the publication *Reality Checks: Teaching Reading Comprehension with Nonfiction* (Stead 2006b).

When I worked with Lauren Benjamin in her first-grade classroom at the Manhattan New School, we linked independent reading with content understandings in our literacy centers as part of reading workshop. When Lauren first established literacy centers, she ensured that independent reading was a core component of each center, similar to those mentioned earlier in the chapter. During the latter part of the year, she included her science unit on living things. Specifically, the children were exploring ants, ladybugs, fish, and tadpoles. She incorporated information about these animals into each center. For example, the Big Book center had about one or more books about these animals. In the listening center, the children were given books about a specific animal. At the computer center, Lauren had websites directly linked to each of the animals.

Lauren also established animal stations where she would have the specific animal together with books and magazines about each creature. In this way, the children could not only read about the animal but also observe it to confirm what they had read. This is an important part of independent reading. We need to encourage children to read informational texts as well as to confirm or question what they have read through direct observations. Unlike fiction, nonfiction can contain incorrect, conflicting, and outdated information. Our learners need experiences in comparing and contrasting what they read with what they observe. At each animal center, children recorded their findings in a notebook based on reading about and directly observing specific animals. As seen in Figure 2.4, the children who read about butterflies

Figure 2.4
Children's Recorded Observations About Butterflies

recorded their comparisons between the information read and the butterflies observed.

Your topic will determine whether such observations are viable. If the class were exploring communities, it may not be possible to have physical items to support content understanding. In these scenarios, media texts such as videos, DVDs, and computer websites can be used to encourage children to compare and to contrast information from what they have read with what they have observed.

In some instances, the children found that information they observed was not mentioned in the books and magazines they read. This led to discussions on how readers look at many different sources to verify their observations. They were told that if they discovered something from an observation but couldn't confirm it in one of the books in the classroom, then they should seek other sources such as the Internet, the school and local public library, or classmates and family members. As seen in Figure 2.5, Mina made an interesting observation about the eating habits of fish but couldn't find this information in any of the books she had read. Undeterred, she went to the school library and even her local library, but none of the books she looked through confirmed her observation. Finally, she decided to cite her book buddy Katie from third grade as a confirmation of her observation. See Figure 2.6. Mina informed me that Katie knew everything about fish and that the authors should have put this into their books because it was, in her words, "interesting stuff that kids need to know."

Figure 2.5
Mina's Observation About Fish

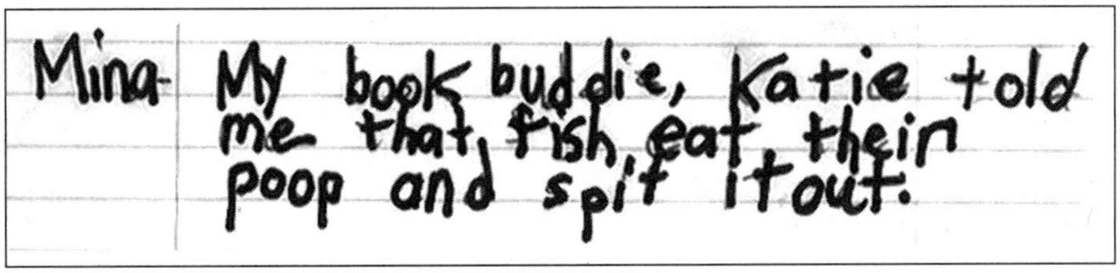

Figure 2.6
Mina Cites Her Source to Confirm Her Initial Observation

Providing Resources

CHAPTER

3

Establishing the Classroom Library

Our classroom library is so cool. We have things on everything kids love. I mean if you like space like me it's here. If I want to read a mystery it's here. When I come in here I just want to sit down and read forever.

Thomas, Grade 3

When I visit schools, I am often amazed by the appearance of many classroom libraries. It is evident that these teachers put much effort into making their classroom libraries colorful and appealing. They are inviting their children to be readers by creating an environment that acts as a magnet to the learner. I have seen everything from a twelve-foot papier-mâché tree for children to grab a book and sit under, to a beach scene complete with beach umbrellas, towels, and beach balls. When I asked the teacher, "Why a beach?" she answered, "Well isn't that where people read?" Mary, a teacher whom I had the pleasure of working with many years ago in Boston, even set up a reading train complete with conductor and train tickets. I really do take my hat off to these teachers; they are perfect salespeople for reading. Unfortunately, these wonderful environments seem to dwindle by third grade and become a long, lost memory by fifth grade. It is always a delight when I happen across fourth- and fifth-grade teachers who continue to provide stimulating and inviting classroom libraries.

Classroom libraries need to be more than a simple collection of trade books. The classroom library is a tool for enhancing children's learning. Not all books need to be on display all the time. You can have a core collection on display all year and then a revolving collection that matches studies and interests.

When libraries are being set up, consider how organizing the books will help children to select reading material freely and easily. Books gathered, sorted, and stored in labeled baskets make them easier for students to retrieve as opposed to packing books tightly on a bookshelf with only the spines visible. The baskets help children to select books and return books to their proper place.

Although aesthetics are important, additional layers need consideration, namely, how we organize the materials in our classroom library, the different forms of literature, such as nonbook materials, that should be available, and the suitability and readability levels of the literature we provide. The next two chapters and Chapter 8 will explore these three issues.

Organizing Materials: Fiction

For many years, I had several baskets of books in my classroom filled with narratives. I simply labeled these baskets "Stories."

At the time, I gave little thought to the specific genre of these texts because I hadn't accumulated a large quantity of materials and my children appeared able to select stories with ease. As I amassed more books, I became aware that during borrowing time my students were taking longer to select texts and were often frustrated. This didn't concern me at first because it took me a long time to make selections at bookstores and the public library.

Only when my student Marisa asked me to help her find some more stories about animals did I reconsider the organization of my literature. Apparently, Marisa had painstakingly gone through the four "Stories" baskets trying to locate books on animals. My book collection

Figure 3.1
Books Housed by Series and Author

had grown into a mini-library and needed to be organized accordingly. I organized the three baskets of stories into categories: "Animal Stories," "Mysteries," and "Adventures." I selected these categories because they were the main genres of my literature. I further created a fourth basket called "Others" to house materials that didn't fit into the other three categories. This was a valuable learning lesson for me. My students were able to select materials more quickly, and I saw that I lacked many other genres.

This realization led me to collect literature in a variety of genres. I also began keeping collections of books together for easy access. When children get hooked on a series such as The Magic Tree House or a favorite author, they want easy access to this material. When I embarked on author studies, it was easier to have all the books by that author together. See Figure 3.1. Each year I found a slightly different way to organize the fiction, which led me to realize that there is no one right method. What is important is that children know where to find materials so that access is simple.

Possible Topics

A multitude of topics could make up the fiction section of a classroom. Figure 3.2 lists some of the possibilities. A classroom library does not have to contain all the titles outlined on this chart. This is only a guide. Depending on students' particular interests, which will undoubtedly vary from grade to grade, different topic and author baskets will need to

Figure 3.2
Possible Topics for
Fiction

Title of Basket or Containers
Mysteries
Adventures
Animal stories
Dinosaur stories
Books by a specific author
Books in a series
Science fiction
Realistic fiction
Friendship
Family
School
Holidays
Good books for buddy reading: *Note:* Two copies of each title should be included.
Fairy tales
Fables
Myths and legends
Poetry
Scary stories
Favorite read-aloud books
Books highly recommended

be established. As outlined later in this chapter, having children involved in the selection process through discussion and completing a survey of interests will be a good guide to this process.

The K/1 Factor

Many of the books in kindergarten and early first grade are almost hybrids of fiction and nonfiction. These early books are frequently written using a fictional person or animal. The structure is either biographical or autobiographical when written in the first person. However, they contain nonfiction information. They often deal with such issues as families, friends, animals, likes, dislikes, games, and hobbies. Take, for example, a book about a duck that has the lines: "I like to swim in the pond. I like to eat worms. I like to dive under the water. I like to play with my brothers and sisters. I like to sleep when it is dark." Technically, this is fictional because it is about an animal that appears to be able to talk and tell us all about the things it likes to do. However, it also contains information about ducks.

My dilemma when I taught kindergarten and first grade was where to place this material. I decided to place the fiction and nonfiction

Figure 3.3
Julie's Classroom
Library

materials on the same topic in the same basket. I had conversations with the children on how we could get lots of facts even from stories. It was only when I began amassing large quantities of materials on a specific topic that I put all the purely informational texts into a separate basket to distinguish between fiction and nonfiction. In Julie Ramos's kindergarten classroom where I consulted, we first decided not to distinguish between our fiction and nonfiction materials. Julie had only been teaching for a few years and didn't have an abundance of books. Most of the material she had was written in the hybrid style as mentioned earlier. We decided to use broad headings and include fiction and nonfiction materials under topics of interest. See Figure 3.3.

Info-fiction

How to organize material that contains both fiction and nonfiction is not limited to kindergarten and first-grade settings. An abundance of materials for grades two through five have a mixture of fiction and nonfiction. I refer to these texts as info-fiction. The series The Magic School Bus is a prime example. More of these series are being written, and they are an excellent way of imparting content understandings in an engaging manner. This material can be organized in a number of ways. Take, for example, *Dinosaurs Before Dark* from The Magic Tree House series. This could be placed in a basket called "Magic Tree House Books," in a basket with other adventure stories, in a basket with other dinosaur stories, or with nonfiction books on dinosaurs. It is important to talk with our students so they know how materials are organized. Later in this chapter we will discuss ways to involve our learners in this organizational process.

The Importance of Nonfiction

When we consider informational texts, the classroom library serves a dual purpose. It acts as both a resource for children to read about personal interests and a source of information to support content learning. We need to ensure that enough materials for both purposes are available for our children to read. Although over recent years informational texts have been an important focus, many classroom libraries either lack specific nonfiction materials or have their nonfiction material organized under the one heading titled "Nonfiction." Research by Duke (2000) found that as little as 6.28 percent of classroom libraries in low socioeconomic districts contained informational texts. In high socioeconomic areas, the percentage was still low at 11 percent. Wherever I consult, I always impress upon schools and districts to have classroom libraries with an abundance of nonfiction. When I worked with Lisa Moynihan in her third-grade classroom, we made a considerable effort to make nonfiction a priority. By the year's end, we had a healthy nonfiction classroom library, as seen in Figure 3.4.

Figure 3.4
Lisa's Nonfiction
Classroom Library

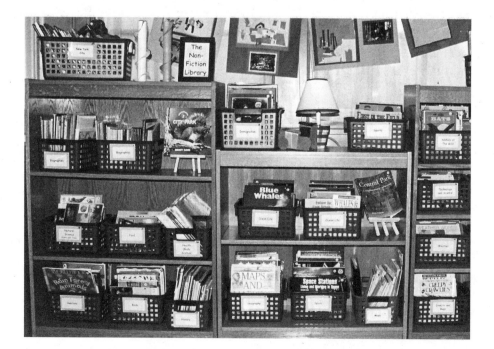

Good Choice!

Nonfiction as Pleasure Reading

Although my son is an avid reader, he often complains about the amount of reading he has to get through in a chapter book; yet, he will happily read for hours on end if he is reading a sports magazine or instructions for a game or a model. Like many children and adults, he enjoys browsing in nonfiction. To him and to so many other children, reading nonfiction is pleasurable. This notion is often contrary to what is happening in many classrooms, where nonfiction reading is viewed purely for the purpose of completing set tasks and projects, and the novel or chapter book is the preferred choice for pleasure.

I periodically look through the best seller's list in the *New York Times*, and I am not surprised to find that nonfiction books are a substantial component of the top ten. The range of books is extensive, from how to be fit and healthy for life to countless biographies that capture our imagination. Nonfiction reading is pleasure reading for many adults and children. This belief is further confirmed when I think about my journeys on the New York subway. It is an expedition that always amazes me. It's another world down there, and I can't help but look at people and wonder about their lives. My New York friends have informed me that this can be a dangerous occupation and that it would be wise to bring a book and keep my eyes on the pages and not on the commuters. Evidently that is exactly what most travelers do, and recently I have become fascinated not by the people, but by what they are reading. For the most part, they are absorbed in newspapers, biographies, and magazines. These magazines are filled with how to look better, feel better, make money, sports results, and reviews of movies, theaters, and restaurants. In other words, the real world, the world of nonfiction. I am certainly not negating the power of fiction or suggesting that children should not, or do not want to, engage in this form of reading. This needs to be encouraged; however, it is only one form of pleasure reading and other forms, specifically nonfiction, need to be unlocked for all our learners.

Nonfiction to Support Content Learning

I believe in linking my language program with my content-specific curriculum. It is critical for teachers to consider their content areas and the units of study they are implementing over the course of the year. This will give a valuable insight into the range of nonfiction materials they will need for their classroom library. Often we expect children to conduct research in a content area only to find a lack of resources inside the

Figure 3.5
Possible Topics for
Nonfiction and Related
Genres

Title of Basket or Container	Text Type/Genre
Animals: Could also be on a specific animal	Descriptive
Space	Descriptive
The ocean	Descriptive
Plants	
Trees	
Dinosaurs	Descriptive
Countries	Descriptive
Places	
Transportation	Descriptive
Reptiles	Descriptive
Birds	Descriptive
Creepy crawlies	Descriptive
Fish	Descriptive
Sports	Descriptive
Hobbies	Descriptive
Celebrations	Descriptive
People and culture	Descriptive
Buildings and structures	Descriptive
Food and recipes	Descriptive/procedural
How to make	Procedural
How to care for	Procedural
How to do	Procedural
How to grow	Procedural
Puzzles and games	Procedural
Atlases and maps	Procedural
Experiments	Procedural
How and why	Explanation
Weather	Descriptive/explanation
Water	Descriptive/explanation
Soil	Descriptive/explanation
Matter	Descriptive/explanation
Energy	Descriptive/explanation
Biographies	Retell
History	Retell
Pioneer days	Retell
Disasters	Descriptive/retell
What do you think?	Persuasive
Catalogues	Persuasive
Poetry	All genres

classroom. Discuss these topics with the school librarian so that books can be borrowed from the school library and placed in the classroom library for the duration of the unit. In Paula Kingston's second-grade class, the children were studying plants as part of a science unit. She set up several baskets of books to assist her children with research. Many of these books were on loan from the school library.

Possible Topics

Although topics selected will be dependent on student's particular interests and units of study in the content areas, we also need to include materials that will broaden student's reading repertoire. If we rely only on children's current interests and content studies, we run the risk of not extending children's reading. Usually most of our nonfiction materials in our classroom libraries focus on descriptions and deal specifically with animals, plants, and space. In my publication *Is That a Fact? Teaching Nonfiction Writing* (2002), I highlighted Andrea's second-grade classroom in which she had numerous baskets of reading materials about topics that deal with not only descriptions but also a range of different text types.

Since then, I have added to the array of possible topics and specific genres that could be included to expand both children's interests and content understandings. See Figure 3.5. It needs to be stressed that a classroom library does not have to contain all the titles outlined on this chart. This is only a guide.

Finding Out Children's Interests

Uncovering children's interests can be easily obtained through whole-class discussions or by giving them a survey of interests as seen in Figure 3.6. See Appendix J for an example. It is crucial to give children a say in what constitutes their classroom library. As teachers, we often do much of the organization of the classroom library and present children with the final product. Our learners are therefore the recipients of what we think the relevant topics for their independent reading should include. It is no different than taking a child to a local public library and telling him or her to borrow materials from specific sections that we have pre-determined as appropriate. Learning at its optimum is when the student takes responsibility for learning.

Survey of Interests

Name Brooke Ryan

Grade 3 3/4 sk

Put an X next to your favorite topics.

Animals	X	Insects	X	Space	
Dinosaurs	X	Sports		Reptiles	X
The Sea		The Ocean		Countries	
Experiments	X	Making Things	X	Famous People	
Adventure Stories		Science Fiction		Mysteries	X
Weather		Plants		Scary Stories	X
Birds		Sports Biographies		Music	
Creepy Crawlies	X	Legends		Fables	
Games and Puzzles		Fairy tales		Food	X

What other topics do you like to read about?

Pets   Dog's

Figure 3.6
Brooke's Survey of Interests

In Jane Carlo's fourth-grade class, we gave the children the survey and informed them that we would use this as a guide when purchasing new materials for the classroom library. Instantly, the children's eyes lit up. "Do you mean we can buy books on stuff we like?" asked Alison. Our learners had become empowered, and this was evident by the barrage of questions they asked. "Can we help buy the books?" pleaded Jose. "What about magazines? Can we buy them too?" inquired Cynthia. When we look at Brooke's survey of interest (Figure 3.6), we can see that she loves reading about a variety of topics, including dogs, dinosaurs, and mysteries. Jane found that her students typically selected materials from these three topics, so she established baskets of reading materials on these topics. Many of the children were also interested in the ocean, which as it happened, was an upcoming science unit. When Jane told the children about the new basket of literature on the ocean and that the class was going to explore this topic as a unit of study, they were excited. The survey of interests had acted as a wonderful link between children's interests and Jane's content teachings.

In Mandy Carlson's kindergarten classroom, it was easier to gather the children together and ask them what they were interested in. Mandy then listed these topics on a chart and set up her interest topic baskets accordingly.

Alternatively, a simpler version of the survey of interest can be given out for children to complete. Kay Marscope asked her kindergartners to draw their interests, and then she recorded these on each child's survey. See Figure 3.7. An example can be found in Appendix K.

Encouraging Children to Assist with the Organizational Process

Once fiction or nonfiction topics have been decided, children can be part of the organizational process. Lisa Moynihan paired students together and gave them one or more empty baskets with the names of the selected topics. For example, Harry and Steven had the "New York City" basket and the "Mysteries" basket. Each pair then decided who was the seeker of materials and who was the keeper. The role of the seeker was to locate materials to include in their baskets. The role of the keeper was to put the resources found by the seeker into the relevant basket. Each seeker and keeper wore a tag to signify their designation. Harry wore a tag that said "Seeker of Mysteries and New York City." Steven wore a tag that said "Keeper of Mysteries and New York City." Lisa had come up with the idea of

Figure 3.7
Hayley's Survey of
Interests

seekers and keepers from the Harry Potter series. Her children loved these books, and she noticed that many of them were discussing the game of Quidditch, in which teams were made up of seekers and keepers. Her use of the children's interest to act as springboard for organizing the classroom library was brilliant.

Lisa placed all the classroom reading materials into the center of the room and asked the seekers to begin searching. The task was simple: Try to locate literature on your topics and give it to your keeper. Before letting her children embark on this mission, she had conversations with them on their roles and responsibilities:

The Role of the Seeker

- Find materials that you think should belong in your topic baskets.
- If you are unsure, give the material to your keeper and let them make the decision.
- If you find materials that belongs in another pair's basket, give it to their seeker.
- Take time to look at the material. Don't just make decisions based on the cover.
- If it is a story, read the blurb to see what kind of story it is, for example, mystery, adventure, science fiction.

The Role of the Keeper

- Look at the materials your seeker gives you to make sure they belong in your baskets.
- Take time to look at the material. Don't just make decisions based on the cover.
- If you find you have too much material see whether any of it could fit into a different category and give it to that keeper.

It was amazing to watch her children in action. It was chaotic, but it was organized chaos. Within twenty minutes, 80 percent of the books and magazines had been organized. What remained was literature that didn't fit into any of the designated categories; therefore, new baskets were established to house this material. The children noticed that many of their baskets were overflowing with materials, whereas others had fewer materials. This led to discussions on subdividing categories that had an abundance of materials and purchasing new materials for categories that were spartan.

Lisa found that giving responsibility to her learners for setting up the classroom library had numerous advantages. It encouraged her learners to take care of their resources because they had been responsible for its organization. It gave her children an opportunity to become immersed in the literature available through browsing. And finally it saved her countless hours in attempting to organize the materials alone. The big decision that Lisa had to make was whether to repeat this process at the beginning of each school year. This would mean totally dismantling the classroom library at the end of each year. For Lisa, this was a simple decision. The seeker and keeper activity had been so valuable in giving her students voice that she decided to repeat the process every year.

The K/1 Factor

Although having children help organize the classroom library is desirable, it can be a difficult process for young learners. Many children in earlier grades can struggle with identifying which materials belong in which topic baskets. Consequently, attempting Lisa's process can be confusing. In Mandy's kindergarten classroom, we found it easier for us initially to place most of the materials in baskets. We then gave each child one or two texts to add to the collection. As new material was purchased for the classroom library, we would ask the children in which topic basket it should be placed. This still allowed them to be part of the organizational process but in a manageable way.

Ensuring That Books Go Back into the Right Basket

I remember one year spending countless hours setting up the classroom library with my children and celebrating its completion. I then encouraged my learners to borrow from the collections and was horrified to find that within a week many of the books and magazines were in the wrong baskets. What I hadn't considered was that my children needed to know how to put materials back in the correct baskets. I learned my lesson quickly. I assigned a number to each basket and placed this number on a stick-on dot on the back of each book. In Lisa's third-grade classroom, each keeper placed stick-on dots on the back of the materials given to them by their seekers. As seen in Figure 3.8, the "New York City" basket has been assigned the number 25. Therefore, Steven, the keeper, wrote the number 25 on each dot and placed it on the back of all the material that belonged in that basket.

Figure 3.8
The New York City Basket with Corresponding Number

Keeping a Record of Classroom Library Topics

Once a classroom library has been established, children will need a quick reference to see what choices are available. One way is to hang a chart in the classroom library listing the available topics, as shown in

Figure 3.9
A List of Topics in the
Classroom Library

Our Class Library

1. Biography
2. Apple Chapter Books
3. Mystery
4. Easy Chapter Books
5. Advanced Chapter Books
6. Fairy Tales
7. Beverly Cleary
8. Classics & Newberry Award Winners
9. Animal Stories
10. Dinosaur Information
11. Outer Space
12. Weather Information
13. Picture Books
14. Historical Fiction
15. Sports Books
16. Plants & Flowers
17. Poetry
18. Folk Tales & Legends
19. Holiday Stories
20. Baby Sitters Club
21. Wonders of the Earth
22. Our Bodies
23. Picture Books
24. Social Studies
25. Fables
26. Information Books
27. Animals In The Wild

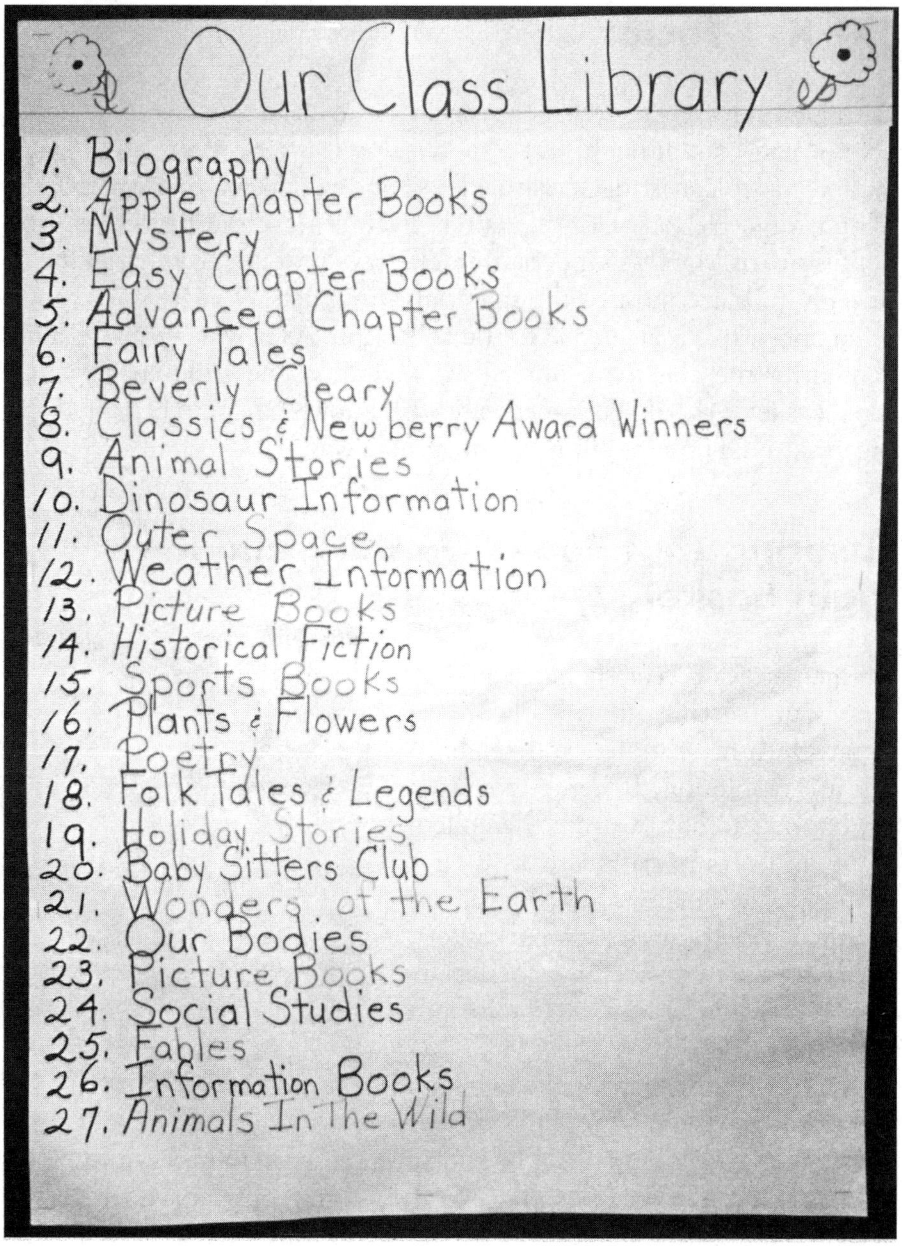

Figure 3.9. In kindergarten and first-grade classrooms, include pictures or symbols next to the name and number of each topic for easy identification. In Katie's kindergarten classroom, we put a picture of a bear on the chart next to the word "animals." For the Space basket, we had a picture of a planet. Many of Katie's children were beginning readers and unable to read the chart, so including pictures made identification possible. Katie and I further decided to put the matching pictures on the label of each basket in the classroom library. This proved to be success-

ful since it enabled the children to look at the chart first and then find the matching topic basket using only the picture. We needed to provide whole-class mini-lessons on what each picture represented so that they understood that the bear symbol meant that the materials were about animals.

I am often asked whether the fiction and nonfiction libraries should be in separate sections of the classroom library. If our classroom libraries are to mirror school and public libraries, then, yes, they need to be separate. However, I really don't think this matters as long as children know where to find reading materials based on interests and research. As seen in Figure 3.9, the fiction and nonfiction topics are organized randomly because Franca, the fifth-grade teacher, let her students organize each basket. In her words, "It's their classroom library; they can organize it any way they like."

Overcoming Shortages of Materials

If we want our students to be readers, then we need materials for them to read. As a builder needs supplies to construct a house, a teacher needs materials to build lifelong readers. Funding for classroom libraries always concerns teachers, and, although they agree that their classroom libraries need to contain a wide range of materials, the cost of purchasing a large quantity of books makes this difficult. One inexpensive way to furnish a classroom library is to include nonbook resources, which will be addressed in the next chapter. There are also other means of building up materials for the classroom library. Over the past twenty years, I have been amazed by the creative and unique ways schools are stocking their classroom libraries. Some of these include:

- Locating existing books/materials in the school
- Sharing resources
- Books from the library
- Garage/lawn sales/markets
- Corporate sponsors
- Donations
- Creative use of funds
- Grants

Nonbook Resources

I love reading magazines because they have so many different things to read about. It's nice because you can just look through them and find interesting articles. I learn lots from reading magazines.

Fiona, Grade 5

Beyond Books

Over the past several years, there has been a growing realization about the importance of providing children with a range of reading materials. As David Booth (2006) pointed out, we need to consider the new literacies that include magazines, journals, newspapers, and other nonbook formats. Many teachers struggle with the concept of incorporating these forms into the classroom library. Gabrielle Martinez, a second-grade teacher in New York, once told me that unless her children have a book in their hands she doesn't feel that they are really reading. I asked Gabrielle to make a list of the materials she had read over the previous week. She was surprised to realize that books constituted only 20 percent. Her reading life was filled with magazines, newspapers, and, not surprisingly, the Internet. Refer to Chapter 5 for a detailed account on how the Internet can be used as part of children's independent reading.

I asked Gabrielle whether she considered these nonbook formats as reading and whether she enjoyed reading these materials. Right away I saw the realization in her expression. She said that she had never considered using nonbook resources during independent reading because she hadn't valued them or even considered them. Gabrielle had been teaching for many years and had always used books as her main reading resource. She had never considered that in today's society we read many different materials and that books were only one of these resources. I am not suggesting that the classroom library should be filled primarily with nonbook resources. Books will still constitute the majority of materials; however, if we want our students to be confident and competent life-long readers for a variety of purposes, then nonbook resources need to be a component of our classroom libraries. In this chapter, we will consider ways to incorporate nonbook resources into the classroom.

Magazines

Magazines are an important component of our independent reading. They are plentiful and cover many topics. According to Rucker's research (1982), reading magazines does have an impact on strengthening students' reading abilities. Magazines written specifically for children can be used in the classroom library. Because these magazines may deal with more than one topic, I purchase multiple copies for the topic baskets. A magazine may have information about both animals and ocean life. By purchasing two copies, I can place one in the "Animal" basket and the other in the "Oceans" basket. Many children's magazines have a game, a recipe, or something to construct. I tear these out of the magazine, paste them onto a large card, and then place them in the relevant topic basket. A crossword puzzle, for example, would be placed in the Puzzles and Games basket. Many magazines are not purely informational. They also contain stories and poems, so again these can be placed into the relevant fiction topic basket. Figure 4.1 lists a sample of magazines that can be incorporated into the classroom library. For each magazine, I have included the appropriate grade level or ages and a web-

Name of Magazine	Ages/Grades	Website
Time for Kids	Separate Issues for K–1, 2–3 & 4–6	http://www.timeforkids.com/TFK
Nickelodeon	All ages	http://www.nick.com
Cricket	Ages 9–14	http://www.cricketmag.com/home.asp/
Pack-O-Fun	All ages	http://www.craftideas.com
Sports Illustrated for Kids	Grades 3–6	http://www.sikids.com
AppleSeeds	Grades 2–5	http://www.cobblestonepub.com/magazine/app/
Chirp, Chickadee and Owl	Grades K–3	http://www.owlkids.com
Tony Stead's Real Life Magazines	Grades 3–6	http://www.rosenpublishing.com
Highlights for Children	All ages	http://www.highlights.com
Kids Discover	Grades 1–6	http://www.kidsdiscover.com
Lady Bug	Grades K–2	http://www.cobblestonepub.com/magazine/lyb/
National Geographic Kids	Grades 3–6	http://www.kids. nationalgeographic.com/
Ranger Rick	Grades 2–6	http://www.nwf.org/gowild/
Sesame Street	Pre-K–K	http://www.sesameworkshop.org/sesamestreet/
U.S. Kids	Grades 2–5	http://www.uskidsmag.org
Your Big Back Yard	Grades K–2	http://www.nwf.org/yourbigbackyard/
Plays	All ages	http://www.playsmag.com
Stone Soup	Grades 3–6	http://www.stonesoup.com/
Dig	Grades 4–9	http://www.cobblestonepub.com/magazine/dig/
Cobblestone American History for Kids	Grades 4–9	http://www.cobblestonepub.com/magazine/cob/
American Girl	Grades 3–7	http://www.americangirl.com/agmg/index.html
Boy's Life	Grades 3–6	http://www.boyslife.org
Children's Digest	Grades 5–7	http://www.cbhi.org/magazines/childrensdigest/index.shtml

Figure 4.1
List of Magazines That Could Be Incorporated into the Classroom Library

site link. Although this list is extensive, it does not list all the available magazines. Rather, they are magazines either that I have used or that have been recommended to me by colleagues.

Many schools/classrooms subscribe to particular magazines, and the children are each given a copy to take home. I was in one of the classrooms when the magazines were being distributed to the children. The teacher was obviously at the end of an exhausting day and quickly gave the magazines to her students five minutes before dismissal time. The only instruction was for the children to take the magazines home to keep. Some children jammed them into their already crowded bags, while others held onto them as they were dismissed from the classroom. On my walk to the train station, I was not surprised to find a trail of magazines littering the sidewalk. It reminded me of Hansel and Gretel's trail of bread crumbs dropped after being taken into the deep, dark forest. I doubt the few magazines that survived the journey home were ever read. What a waste of money and of a valuable classroom resource. Instead, placing these magazines in theme baskets in the classroom library based on content would have been a better use of this valuable resource. These magazines would have helped build up the supply of materials in a classroom library that lacked resources. The students could have borrowed these magazines as part of children's take home reading.

In one school where I taught, our grades three and four team pooled our resources. Each of us subscribed to a different magazine and then distributed copies to each team member. I subscribed to *Time for Kids* and ordered twenty-four copies each month. I gave each of my seven team members three copies of the magazine. I then received three copies of each of the magazines subscribed to by my team members. This meant that each month I received three copies from eight different magazines to add to my classroom library. My classroom library soon had a healthy selection of reading material on a multitude of topics. Furthermore, this information was current and easily accessible for my children.

Newspapers

When I am reading through a newspaper, I often happen on an article about a specific person, place, or thing. I cut these out, paste them onto oak tag, laminate them, and place them in the classroom library under the relevant topic. These articles build up quickly, and before long, the classroom library is full of newspaper articles about a myriad of topics. The travel sections of newspapers are particularly beneficial because they often contain updated information about a specific country or place. This is usually more desirable than purchasing books about specific countries that can be costly and with information that is often outdated a year after purchase. As with magazines, subscriptions to particular newspapers written specifically for children can be a valued addition to the classroom library.

Newspaper articles written from a persuasive standpoint are a terrific asset for the classroom library. When I taught fourth and fifth grade, I periodically looked through my local newspaper to find articles or letters to the editor about local, state, or global issues. I cut these out, pasted them onto cardboard, and placed them in a basket called "What Do You Think?" Sometimes I would add notepaper to the article so that my students could write their thoughts after the reading. My students loved reading each other's views about specific issues and would engage in lengthy discussions.

Catalogs

When I first moved to the United States, I was dismayed by the lack of mail I received each day. The only mail that did find its way into my mailbox were advertising catalogs addressed to the former occupants of my house. Ten years later I was dismayed for a different reason: the huge quantities of daily mail that jammed my mailbox, specifically the unending stream of catalogs, catalogs, and more catalogs. They are no longer addressed to some former occupant but to my family and me. Even my thirteen-year-old son receives, on average, one catalog per week. What amazes me is that they are from companies and stores I have never shopped at and, quite frankly, see no impending need to start. For years, I threw these out with the rest of the junk mail, usually behind my wife's back because, unlike me, she finds them compelling and very high-interest reading. However, one day as I gathered a pile of them and made my way to the trash my son picked one up and said, "Papa, we need to buy these things for our kitchen. I think Mama and me will like them." It dawned on me that there was a place for some of these catalogs in the classroom library. If children are to be readers for many purposes, then they need to understand the power of advertising. Advertising is one of the most abundant and influential reading forms that affect our daily decisions in the world of commerce. Millions of people read catalogs for pleasure—even if I am not one of them.

Armed with this newly discovered notion, I quickly set up an interest basket in one of the classrooms where I was working and named it "Shopping." I filled it with catalogs from toy and publishing companies, office supply stores, and sporting stores. I was eager to see whether any of the children would select these during independent reading and to listen to their conversations after selecting such literature. To my delight, they became one of the hottest commodities in the classroom library. Evidently my wife and son were not the only two people who found such reading material compelling. Inside each catalog I placed a piece of paper with specific focuses, as seen in Figure 4.2. I provided these additional focuses because it is essential to guide children's independent reading of such materials for an authentic purpose. The office

Type of Catalog	Instructions
Toys/games	■ What presents do you hope Santa will leave you? Make a list and show it to your parents. (K–2) ■ Which toys do you think are the best? Why do you think this? ■ Write a letter to you parents to convince them why they should buy you a particular toy or game. ■ Make a list of the things you would like for your next birthday. (Grades 3–5)
Food	■ What are your favorite ten foods? Make a list. ■ Which foods do you think are the most healthy? Why do you think they are healthy? ■ Make up a recipe using some of the foods in the catalog.
Supplies	■ What supplies do you think we need for our classroom? Make a list and leave it on your teacher's table. Tell your teacher why you think we should buy them. ■ Which items do you think are too expensive? Why do you think this? ■ Compare the prices of items in different catalogs. Are some cheaper than other?
Publishers	■ Make a list of the books and magazines you think we should have in our classroom library. Give it to your teacher. Tell your teacher why you think we should have these in our classroom library.
Sporting stores	■ Which of these items do you already have at home? Which ones would you like?
Clothing	■ If you could buy ten pieces of clothing, what would they be? ■ Which clothes don't you like? Why don't you like them?
Computer/electronics	■ Which of these would you like for your birthday? ■ Which computer games do you think would be better than others? ■ Compare the prices of items in different catalogs. Are some cheaper than others?

Figure 4.2
Reading Focuses to Go with Specific Catalogs

supply catalogs were particularly popular because I had informed the children that we had been given $100 for classroom publishing supplies and they were eager to spend it.

Cereal/Food Boxes

I am amazed by the amount of information on the back of food boxes, especially cereal boxes. I'm starting to think that the slew of information lodged in my brain, from geographical sites to biographical information about anybody who's anyone, came not from my elementary school education but from the back of the cornflakes box. These food boxes have three major advantages. First, they contain an enormous variety of nonfiction information about a range of topics such as animals, plants, space, countries, people, and places. Second, they are on strong cardboard, which makes them durable and easy to cut out and to place directly in the relevant topic basket in the classroom library. Third and more important, they are free. In one of the classrooms where I worked, the teacher, Melissa Perkins, asked her children to start bringing in cereal and food boxes that had information on the back. Within one month, she had filled her classroom library with wonderful reading materials for her children, and it cost her nothing.

Children's Own Publications: The Reading/Writing Connection

I am a great believer in children publishing as part of writing workshop. When the writer takes his or her piece to publication for others to read, the reading/ writing connection is at its best. I invest in colored paper, markers, oak tag, and binding tapes so that when my children take a particular piece to publication, it looks professional and inviting. After publishing and sharing a particular piece, I invite my students to place their publication in the relevant topic basket for other children to borrow and read during independent reading. See Figure 4.3. It doesn't surprise me to find that these publications are always in demand by my readers. Children love reading each other's writings, especially when these writings are presented in a published format. In my own classroom, each of my children published on average five pieces a year and donated at least two of these to the classroom library. In a class of thirty children, this translated into sixty pieces a year. In three years, I had built up a resource of 180 books for my classroom library.

Figure 4.3
The Basket Titled "Our Publications on Animals" That Contains Children's Published Pieces

Children may wish to place a blank page at the end of their published pieces inviting future readers to sign their names after reading the publication. This gives the reader feedback about the number of people who have read their piece. In classrooms where I have worked I would often catch children running over to the classroom library to see how many of their classmates had read their publications. What pure delight would wash across their faces when they saw other children's names in the back of their publications. In one classroom, Jose asked his readers to inform him whether his book was too easy, too hard, or just right. He later told me that he was going to start writing harder books because, in his words, "Most of my books are too easy for the kids. I need to write some just rights." This is a good example of how our readers can inform our writers.

As seen in Figure 4.4, children can include a page at the back of their publications titled "About the Author." On this page, they can list their name, age, likes, dislikes, and other information about themselves. This is an excellent community-building tool because it gives students the opportunity to read about and make connections with their classmates. The inclusion of information about other books or pieces they have written acts as a way of inviting the reader to read more publications by their peers. Refer to Appendix L for an "About the Author" page you may wish to give to your children to place in the back of their publications.

If we are to include children's own publications in the classroom library, then children need to follow a few guidelines. Through whole-class discussions and mini-lessons, a set of guidelines can be established. The list that follows can be displayed in the classroom. It is useful to first ask the children what makes a good publication for others to read rather than just presenting them with a list of guidelines. This gives them voice, responsibility, and ownership in the learning process. It also helps them produce a set of expectations that they feel are important to meet.

When I taught kindergarten and first grade, I found that many of my young writers struggled to publish their

Figure 4.4
About the Author

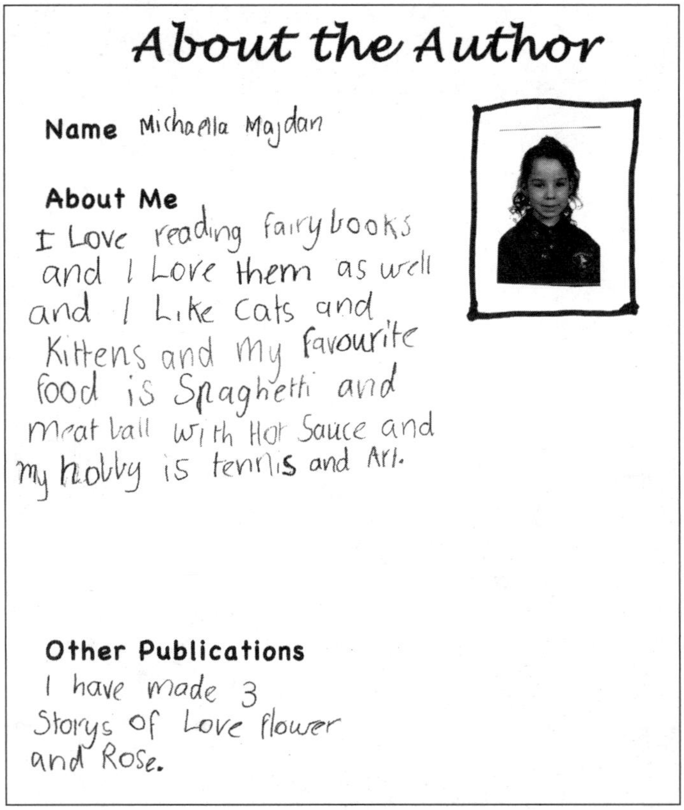

About the Author

Name Michaella Majdan

About Me
I Love reading fairy books and I Love them as well and I Like cats and Kittens and my favourite food is Spaghetti and meat ball with Hot Sauce and my hobby is tennis and Art.

Other Publications
I have made 3 Storys of Love flower and Rose.

pieces legibly so others could easily read them. I therefore had parent helpers type many of the publications the children had selected to place in the classroom library.

What Makes a Good Publication for Our Baskets

- The handwriting is your best and it can be read.
- You have lots of great information.
- The writing is big enough for everyone to read.
- Your publication is interesting.
- There are spaces in between the words.
- There are no spelling mistakes.
- It looks good.
- There are fantastic pictures.
- You are proud of it.

Maps

Whenever I travel on a plane I love to look at the back of the airline magazine to locate the map. Even though I've seen these maps countless times, I'm still fascinated by the different places around the world. Many children share my fascination with maps, whether they are from an atlas, a tourist map pointing out specific scenic routes and landmarks, or a train or bus map. During independent reading time, I've watched my students discuss maps in pairs and locate a myriad of information. Maps are an important component of our functional reading. I found that one of the best ways to teach my children geography was to place multiple copies of maps pertaining to a specific place in a basket in the classroom library for access during independent reading time. I attached a list to particular maps asking children to locate certain landmarks or places. See the following for a map of North America:

Can You Find?

The Mississippi River
San Diego
The state of Maine
The province of Manitoba
The Rio Grande
The Atlantic Ocean
Alaska
Places that begin with the letter *T*
States that are on the East Coast
States that are on the West Coast
States that are completely surrounded by other states

I added this information to a particular map because children need a focus when viewing such material. Giving them a map of, say, Asia and expecting them to locate information and engage in meaningful conversations without guidance may be too difficult, especially for early learners. Chances are they will stare blankly at the map and soon become disengaged. As adults, we usually look at maps to locate specific information so it makes sense for children to do likewise.

Linking these maps to ongoing science and social themes in the classroom is beneficial. Children are able to engage in more meaningful discussion in which they can access and use prior knowledge based on whole-class discussions. In Jennifer Gately's first-grade classroom, the children were studying their neighborhood as part of a social studies unit. Jennifer constructed maps of the local neighborhood and placed multiple copies of these in the basket labeled "Our Neighborhood." This basket also contained brochures, articles, and pictures of the local community. She attached a sheet of paper to each map that asked the reader to locate specific landmarks they had talked about during whole-class discussions. Jennifer used independent reading as an opportunity for her children to not only read to locate new information but also to consolidate existing understandings being taught. For information on how to use maps as part of instruction, refer to Chapter 9 in *Reality Checks: Teaching Reading Comprehension with Nonfiction* (Stead 2006b). Some of the possible maps that could be included in the classroom library are listed next. Based on content, these maps could be placed either in specific topic baskets or in a basket titled "Maps."

Types of Maps

Bus and train maps showing specific routes (These could include schedules.)
Classroom map
Map of the school library
Map of the school
Evacuation maps
Map of the local community
Maps of shopping malls
Atlases
Airline maps
Road maps
Climate maps
Tourist maps
Maps of areas discovered by explorers
Maps of specific states, territories, or provinces
Maps of specific countries

Map of the solar system
Political maps
Maps that show populations in specific regions
Maps of wildlife, endangered species, plants, habitats, etc.

Brochures/Pamphlets

As with maps, brochures and pamphlets are an excellent addition to the classroom library. The local travel agent and the tourist information center, where I pick up brochures and pamphlets, are my greatest resources. Their publications contain a wealth of information about the history, geography, climate, flora, and fauna of places around the world. As with newspaper articles and magazines, brochures and pamphlets are often more desirable than purchasing books. The information is current, and brochures can be easily replaced. Information in books can become outdated after a few years. The added bonus: like cereal boxes, brochures and pamphlets are free.

Students can also produce their own brochures and pamphlets as part of writing investigations. Christina Riska, a fourth-grade teacher in Denton, Texas, had her students produce a persuasive brochure. The children were studying bats as part of a science unit. For their whole-class writing investigation they produced a persuasive brochure that explained why bats are helpful creatures and shouldn't be feared. See Figures 4.5 and 4.6. This brochure made a wonderful addition to the classroom library.

Figure 4.5
Outside of Brochure About Bats

Figure 4.6
Inside of Brochure
About Bats

Bats Are Helpful Creatures

Unfortunately, many people think very badly of bats. Some people even believe horror films that show bats as evil, blood-sucking creatures. As a result, some people are horrified of bats. They should know better! If they don't, by the time they finish reading this brochure they will know the truth about bats and how they are helpful, gentle, and harmless.

Bats are very helpful in many ways. For example, megabats (fruit bats) poop out, or defacate, undigested fruit seeds which plant new fruit trees. In the process of the seed plantation, the bat droppings help enrich the soil. Because of this, the bats help re-seed and maintain the rainforests. Megabats also pollinate flowers with the pollen on their furry snout. The pollen collects on their soft fur as they drink nectar from each flower.

(Left) Bat guano containing undigested seeds helps to re-plant fruit trees. (Right) Bats fly from flower to flower drinking nectar while pollinating them.

Another example of how bats are helpful is that they are believed to guide Native Americans. The ancient Navajo Indians believe that bats are a link between humans and God. The Navajo Indians believe when people pass away, bats guide them to heaven. This legend gives people hope for a better life.

Finally, bats are helpful due to echolocation. Microbats use echolocation to navigate and to hunt insects, fish, and small mammals. Bats sense several things at once with their nose, mouth, and ears. They have excellent hearing as well. When you see a microbat with its mouth open, it's because it is sending out sound waves for echolocation (and NOT to bite someone). Due to echolocation, microbats keep the population of insects under control by preying on them. For example, microbats can usually devour more than 1,200 bugs per hour! Bats can also reduce the chance of disease in animals by eating the insects that carry the diseases.

Megabats (above) and microbats (below) care for their young.

BATS ARE GENTLE AND HARMLESS

Bats are also gentle and harmless. They usually won't hurt people. In fact, bats will only bite you if you try to hurt, startle, or frighten them. Some people believe bats are evil spirits of the night, but they are not. This is a myth. Also, most bats live away from humans because they are more terrified and intimidated of us than we are of them.

Another example of gentleness is that vampire bats do not hurt animals when they drink their blood. The animals do not feel it when the bat bites them because it is a miniscule (5mm) cut.

This megabat is re-seeding fruit trees with its droppings.

Since bats are so gentle, they are much like us in that they are good parents who take care of their young. Female bats are very caring mothers. Microbat mothers take care of their babies in nurseries. Megabat mothers carry their babies with them. This shows how nurturing bats are.

Bats are also harmless mammals. For example, they are clean animals that spend most of their time grooming. Very few bats carry rabies, but you should always remember this rule: Never handle a bat or any other wild animal. Remember, bats are gentle and harmless!

BATS ARE INTERESTING AND GRACEFUL

Bats are also interesting and graceful mammals. In fact, they are the only mammals that can fly on earth. They use their wings to pull themselves through the air. They fly to keep away from predators.

Did you know there are many other interesting facts about bats? One is that bats are not blind. However, in addition to their eyes, bats also use echolocation to get around and hunt for their food. The Pallid Bat echolocates to catch its prey and gets its water from the insects it eats. Another interesting fact is that some bats are good crawlers and leapers. The vampire bat even leaps to its prey! In addition, bat babies are born alive and not in eggs. Baby bats weigh 25% of their mother's weight. Lastly, many bats are endangered. Let's protect them!

This microbat is echolocating to find its food.

Pictures/Photographs

What a wonderful resource a picture or photograph can be for independent reading as long as we accept the idea that reading is not just written print. Visual literacy, as it is sometimes referred to, is a powerful medium for giving a reader information and one that needs to be part our independent classroom libraries. I recently placed in a second-grade classroom library a book of pictures about Australia for children to enjoy during independent reading. I watched as two children eagerly borrowed the book and engaged in complex discussions that covered the topics of landscapes, animals and their habitats, people, food, and recreation. They were totally absorbed in the book, and at the end of independent reading time, they had gathered an incredible amount of information about my homeland.

I also encourage children to bring in photographs, postcards, and pictures from home that are relevant to a specific topic to add to the interest baskets. These include landscapes, buildings, flora, fauna, transportation vehicles, and machinery. I ask the children to place these in clear plastic pockets for protection and to write their names on the back so they remember which pictures they own. I also invite them to write a small message on the back of the picture or on an attached sheet of paper so the reader can find out more after looking at the picture.

Maryanne, a third grader, bought in a picture of a cheetah she had cut out of a magazine. On an attached sheet of paper she wrote, "This animal is a cheetah. Did you know it can run faster than any other animal? If you find out more information write it on this page."

Procedural Guides

The ability to read and to comprehend procedures is crucial. Procedural reading should be part of children's independent reading; however, it needs to be placed in a real context. Children reading about how to make a paper kite or how to build a castle out of LEGOs without actually engaging in the process makes no sense. I recently watched two children following a set of instructions on how to make a paper plane. Not only did they need to read the instruction carefully, but they also needed to reread many of the directions repeatedly when they found their own construction didn't resemble the one pictured in the set of instructions. I doubt these children would have spent this amount of rereading if they were not actually constructing the plane. Therefore, have materials on hand. Some examples of procedural guides may include:

- Recipes
- Origami
- Caring for a class pet
- How to clean the classroom
- How to tie your shoelaces
- Directions to the school office from the classroom
- How to make a kite
- How to make a paper plane
- Making clothes out of paper
- Science experiments
- How to grow plants, for example, carrots, potatoes, radishes, wheat
- How to make different colors with paint using only the primary colors
- How to draw or make different shapes
- How to write different letters of the alphabet
- How to draw different animals
- How to use a computer
- How to play a specific game
- How to find out how tall you are
- How to find out what size your foot is
- How to make a birthday card

Procedural guides are not only limited to construction activities, games, and puzzles but are also a valuable component of this genre. Kathy King, an accomplished fourth-grade teacher with a particular interest in hands-on mathematics, has a comprehensive collection of game boards, puzzles, and quizzes. It was while watching her children one day during the mathematics period that it dawned on me to use some of these games for independent reading and to make them part of the classroom library. I watched as two of her students engaged in a board game that required them to pick up cards and ask each other questions. The board game also required them to follow a set of instructions when their marker landed on a particular square. These children were spending most of their time reading, specifically following instructions, and yet they were two children who disliked reading. This was purposeful and engaging reading to them. I am not saying that board games should make up all of children's independent reading; however, they have a place outside of the mathematics period.

Independent Reading and the Computer

A s the importance and reliance on computers grows in our changing society, so do the implications of how to use this technology effectively in the classroom. Children need to be competent in using this media if they are to be successful in life. Whereas the book was once the major medium, especially for research, the computer has now become an equal resource for gaining information about the world. However, the computer is not just a tool for research. It is also a form of pleasure reading and as such needs to be a core component of both child-selected reading, as outlined in Chapter 1, and teacher-directed reading encounters, as discussed in Chapter 2.

The number of computers available will determine the extent to which this resource can be used for both pleasure reading and research. I have worked in schools in which every child has access to a computer.

Some schools have computer labs where children receive quality time and instruction in using this valuable resource. Unfortunately, I have also worked in classrooms with one outdated computer sitting in the corner with limited or no access to the Internet. In this scenario, a teacher can do little to incorporate this resource into instruction. It is like trying to teach reading with only one book. My hope is that within the next decade all children will have access to and learning experiences with the Internet. It is, without a doubt, the most remarkable new literacy of our times. Students who are skilled in this technology will have a clear advantage over those who are not.

Using the Computer for Pleasure Reading

Over the course of the week, during independent reading time, each child should have the opportunity to use the computer to read about topics of interest. Although during independent reading time, students ultimately need to be responsible for selecting their own materials, if they access the computer without guidance, they will spend their time browsing websites, engaging in little or no reading. Many websites are inappropriate in both content and readability levels. To alleviate these concerns, I initially locate websites for them myself by initiating discussions on topics of interest as outlined in Chapter 1 and then locating appropriate websites for them to visit. Once I have found these websites, I make a list, and each week I bookmark three or four of them on the computer. At the beginning of each week, I inform the children about which websites are available for them to visit during independent reading time. At first, I bookmarked all the websites I had found, but there were too many, and consequently, the children spent their time deciding which website to visit rather than reading.

Computer Games and Independent Reading

In *Even Hockey Players Read*, David Booth (2002) presents some convincing arguments on the importance of the computer as part of children's independent reading. Specifically, he outlines why computers need to be an integral part of any reading program. He also raises the issue of how boys tend to view the computer, specifically computer games, as far more pleasurable than reading a good book. This is the case with my son. Although he is an avid reader of good books, playing games on the computer at night is far more enjoyable for him. I fought the notion that computer games were a valued form of reading, but I realize that they play an important role in his literacy development. Indeed, research by Professor James Paul Gee (2004) of the University of Wisconsin and David Williamson Shaffer (2006) demonstrates the intricate and complex literacy skills that can be learned and developed from these games.

This leaves me with the question, Should these games play a part of independent reading? Although I acknowledge the power of computer games and accept that they are a form of pleasure reading, especially for boys, I also realize that independent reading time may not be the best time for playing games. Independent reading time gives students access to reading their favorite materials. It broadens their reading repertoire and builds up reading stamina. Given that many children have computers at home and will play computer games after school, independent reading time should be reserved for promoting the reading of a running piece of text. Students can play appropriate computer games during free time or after finishing tasks. Depending on the game, they can also be a useful tool in math.

Using the Computer for Research

With the Web expanding at a staggering rate, the computer is the keeper of more information than all of the libraries in the world combined. With access comes not only a wealth of valuable information that can be used in the classroom but also a host of problems in trying to access and locate accurate and relevant information. For many years, I was almost too frightened to use the computer as a research tool because it seemed to present more problems than successes. There were too many websites to navigate. However, if I am organized and put in some preliminary groundwork, then it can be a valued resource in the classroom. Some suggestions follow.

Locating Relevant Websites

Children need to learn how to locate websites for research. This is an ongoing process. Children will need many demonstrations and learning experiences. I therefore find it best to do the groundwork myself initially and gradually release the responsibility to my learners. The age and background experiences of the students will determine the amount of support needed to lead them to independence. First I identify the units of study in science and social studies in which students will be required to research. I make a list of three or four relevant websites for each topic. I limit these website to only three or four per unit because I find this is a good starting point and that listing all the relevant websites for each unit would take months. It is better to have three or four excellent websites than twenty mediocre ones. In identifying these websites I consider their readability levels, accuracy and, more important, the relevance of the information. It would be useless to include a website that had information about a topic that wasn't directly linked to my science and social studies goals. If animal habitats were one of the science topics for investigation, then it would be pointless to have websites that deal primarily with food chains and physical attributes of specific animals if there were no links to their habitats.

When considering the readability of websites, I look for information that most of my children can easily read and understand. If websites are challenging, the children will resort to copying the information. Using the computer to independently read and locate information is not about being challenged when it comes to decoding the text. It is about being able to easily read information to confirm prior thinking and locate new information. To determine whether readability levels are suitable for students, I let students review the websites. I select children who are reading just under grade level to assist me with this task. If these children can read and understand the sites I have identified, then it is logical to assume that, apart from my struggling readers, most of my students will be successful in retrieving information. To assist struggling readers, I pair them with more able students who can easily navigate the selected websites.

To overcome the daunting task of finding relevant websites for the science and social studies topics to be explored over the course of the year, I find that working as a team with other teachers of the same grade level makes light work of a seemingly endless task. If each teacher is responsible for one or two topics, related websites can be easily shared. A comprehensive list of great websites directly linked to specific topics can be found at the end of this chapter.

Blocked websites are another consideration when trying to locate relevant sites. Most districts where I have worked have filters, and at times, and for no apparent reason, these filters can block valuable websites. Although this is frustrating, it is best that you locate accessible sites. These filters protect our children from inappropriate information and images; therefore, it is important to keep them in place.

Accessing and Updating Information

Once relevant websites have been identified, children access these by either bookmarking them onto a favorites page on the Internet browser or copying and saving relevant information into a Word document on the desktop. I find that the latter is especially useful if the website is slow in loading or children are having difficulties connecting to the Web. Saved documents give children instant access to information by simply opening the document. This is helpful with children who have never used the Internet or who have limited computer skills.

I encourage children to try to locate additional websites throughout the unit of study, and if appropriate, I add these to my original list. This is how I build up a substantial collection. Monitoring the websites to ensure they are still relevant and at suitable readability levels is imperative. I replace dated sites with those that are current and easy to navigate. If I find I have amassed too many sites, then I cull these to a reasonable number so that my children won't become overwhelmed.

The K/1 Factor

For many pre-emergent and early emergent readers, the Web can be a daunting prospect. Most websites on specific topics are designed for children who can already read. Some websites such as streaming. discoveryeducation.com include short video clips on specific topics and are an excellent way for young learners to gain information by reading visuals rather than words. If a parent helper, teacher's aide, or assistant is available, he or she can work with individuals or a small group and read information from a website. If such support is not available, then providing audio to match printed information on websites is another option. To accomplish this, save relevant information into a document and use a program such as SimpleText to provide the audio. Another possibility is to create your own website with audio.

If each teacher in the grade area locates websites for only one or two topics and provides the necessary audio, then these files can be shared, making the process quick and efficient.

Helping Children Locate Websites Independently

Although at first I provide children with relevant websites, the ultimate goal is for my learners to be able to locate their own. This is a complex process and many demonstrations are required. Children in kindergarten, first grade, and second grade struggle with this process; therefore, it is best that I lay the groundwork, as described earlier in this chapter. For children in grades three through six, careful scaffolding in whole-class, small-group, and individual settings can lead them to successfully navigate the intricacies of independent Web surfing.

In Patty Davison's sixth-grade classroom in Melbourne, Australia, where I have been working, we assisted her learners through a series of demonstrations and learning experiences as part of a social studies unit on "People and Culture." The children first needed to know what words to type into one of the many search engines such as Safari, Google, Yahoo!, or Internet Explorer so that relevant websites could be located. We were specifically studying China as part of the social studies unit, so we typed in the word *China* into a designated search engine. The children were amazed that 741 million websites were available. We explained that when we typed the word *China* into the search engine it located all the websites that contained this word either in the title or in the first few lines of available information. We also showed them that "China" had been highlighted in boldface on the websites. We examined the first four pages of the listings and found that the websites centered on different topics, including history, culture, food, economics, animals, plants, maps, specific provinces, and a host of other categories. Some websites had little to do with the country China. These were about plates, bowls, and tea sets made from china. This was an eye-opener for the children, and they realized that we would need to be more specific.

Next we asked the children what we really wanted to find out about China. We reminded them that this unit was specifically focused on similarities and difference between the people of China and the people of Australia with respect to culture. We made a list as follows:

Things We Need to Find Out About in Chinese Culture

- Schools
- Recreation
- Food
- Clothing
- Music
- Sports
- Hobbies
- The arts

We then started with the first category, "schools," and asked the children what we should type into the search engine. After a discussion, the children decided that the best words to use were "All about China and its schools." We followed their instructions and 154 million websites were identified. Many of these sites seemed random and dealt primarily with specific schools and happenings on their campuses. Few websites appeared to deal with the Chinese education system. We showed the children that in addition to the keywords *China* and *schools*, the words *all* and *about* had also been highlighted in bold in both the names of the website and the brief descriptions.

This led to discussions about the importance of key words and, specifically, nouns and verbs. The children realized that too much information can result in too many random websites and that each word had to be key. Interestingly, when we typed the phrase "All about China and its schools" into the search engine, the right-hand side of the web page listed sponsored links. One was titled "Education in China." Patty and I explained that sponsored links were commercial links in which you could purchase journals, magazines, and books about the subject matter or join a specific organization. We asked the students whether they thought the phrase "Education in China" was more specific than what we had used. We decided to use these words and found 299 million websites; however, the website on the first page primarily focused on the schooling system in China. We had hit the jackpot!

Patty and I continued the discussions with the children by looking more closely at the websites we had found. We opened a few of these sites and the children found that they were too complex to understand.

We informed the children that we would need to look through the list to locate a website that contained not only relevant information but also information we could read and understand. We eventually located a few and saved these into a favorites page on the Web browser.

At this point, Patty and I decided to end the session, but not before reflecting with the children on what we had learned so far about locating specific websites. Our conclusions are in the list that follows:

How to Locate Websites
- Think about what it is you really want to find out.
- Make a list of key words.
- Try to use only nouns and verbs.
- Look at the first page of the websites listed to see whether they are about what you are looking for.
- If they are not, look for key words on the websites listed and the sponsored links to help make your searches more specific.
- Once you have located websites, open them to see that the information is relevant and can be easily read and understood.

The following day Patty and I gave the children a chance to practice what we had demonstrated the day before. We arranged access to seven computers and put the students into groups of four. We gave each group one of the categories from the list we had created about what we wanted to find out about Chinese culture and then asked them to try to locate relevant websites using the points on the chart as a guide. Patty and I used this time to roam around the classroom assisting students as needed. We were not surprised to find that many students struggled with the task. Most of them did not have computers at home and had little experience surfing the Web. We knew we would have to provide ongoing support for these learners since this was a complex process.

With continued support, most of Patty's students were able to locate relevant websites independently. The major challenge was not finding the relevant sites but rather locating those that they could actually read and understand. Children in early to middle primary grades need to have appropriate websites targeted for them. If it is challenging for sixth graders, then it is nearly impossible for less experienced learners. Interestingly, when I've worked with students who have computers at home, locating relevant sites can also be a struggle. When I interviewed thirty fifth- and sixth-grade students and asked them which sites they viewed at home and how they located these, they said music and game sites were their prime viewings and that they knew about these websites from friends. Few of these children used search engines. They relied primarily on sites recommended to them by their peers. This would support the notion that all children need continual scaffolds regardless of whether they own a computer.

Authenticating the Accuracy of Websites

Assisting children with identifying appropriate websites by using a search engine and then looking for sites that they can understand is only part of the equation. We also need to consider the accuracy of the information presented in a website. Regarding accuracy, books have an advantage over the Web. For the most part, the contents of a book contain accurate information and are published by experts in the field. Some of the information may contain conflicting views, but mostly, information on topics relevant to children in elementary school will be accurate and consistent with other publications on that theme. The Web, however, is a different story. Anyone can be the author of a website regardless of his or her expertise on a given topic. However, most websites written specifically for elementary schoolchildren are by people who have a base knowledge in the subject matter.

To assist students with locating authentic and reliable websites, I instruct them to look for sites by organizations, which are indicated by ".org" rather than ".com." I also encourage them to compare and contrast information from different sites. If they find a website that presents information consistent with other websites, then there's a good chance that the information is reliable.

Finding and Recording Specific Information

Once websites have been identified and saved either into a favorites page or on the desktop, it is important that children know what information they are searching for when reading specific sites. Often these sites contain a wealth of information and children can forget what they are looking for when researching. This happens to me when I surf the Web. Even though I may have specific information in mind that I'm searching for, I can become easily distracted by other information I'm reading and have to remind myself what it was I was looking for in the first place. Focused graphic organizers are a great means to assist children accomplish this goal.

In Helen Jamison's second-grade class, the children were exploring animal habitats. To help them locate and record specific information from the websites, I gave each child an organizer such as the one in Figure 5.1. Refer to Appendix M for a sample. For children in kindergarten and first grade, these organizers can still be used but will need to be simplified. For example, the organizer in Figure 5.1 could be adapted to have only three habitats such as water, land, and mountains and include an illustration of each. The children could then draw animals that lived in each of these habitats after viewing selected websites. Chapter 10 also includes organizers that can be used and adapted for children in kindergarten and first grade when locating and recording information from websites.

One organizer that I have used successfully to help children locate specific information is shown in Figure 5.2. I got this idea from Judy Loeper, a third- and fourth-grade teacher from Honey Brook Elementary in the Twin Valley School District in Pennsylvania. Judy used this organizer in guided reading, but I have found it equally effective in helping children locate specific information

Figure 5.1
Organizer for Locating and Recording Specific Information

Name Cindy

These animals live in deserts.	These animals live in the ocean.	These animals live in fresh water.
snakes lizards birds camels scorpiun	wales sharkes fish seahorses jelly fishes	fish turtles frogs snakes
These animals live in trees.	These animals live in jungles.	These animals live in forests.
birds snakes frogs owls spiders	tigers monkeys snakes birds spiders	deers rabbits snakes lizards skunks birds spiders
These animals live under the ground.	These animals live where there's snow.	These animals live in mountains.
worms moles spiders rabbits groundhogs	poler bears pengins seals fox	got goats sheep birds snakes

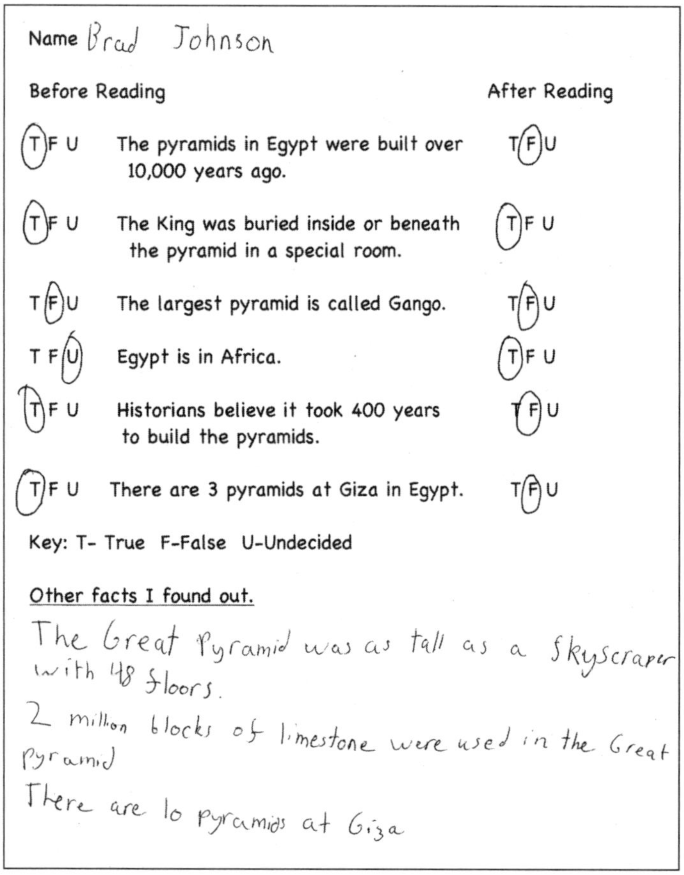

Name *Brad Johnson*

Before Reading   After Reading

(T) F U   The pyramids in Egypt were built over   T (F) U
            10,000 years ago.

(T) F U   The King was buried inside or beneath   (T) F U
            the pyramid in a special room.

T (F) U   The largest pyramid is called Gango.   T (F) U

T F (U)   Egypt is in Africa.   (T) F U

(T) F U   Historians believe it took 400 years   T (F) U
            to build the pyramids.

(T) F U   There are 3 pyramids at Giza in Egypt.   T (F) U

Key: T- True   F-False   U-Undecided

Other facts I found out.

The Great Pyramid was as tall as a skyscraper with 48 floors.

2 million blocks of limestone were used in the Great Pyramid.

There are 10 pyramids at Giza

Figure 5.2
Brad's Organizer for
Reading a Website
About Egypt

from designated websites. Before reading a particular site, students record whether the statements on the organizer are true or false. Students can also select "undecided" if they are unsure. In this way, I am setting up their reading through prediction. It focuses them on the content I want them to look at a website. As children read the information on the site, I ask them whether they can confirm prior thinking or whether they want to change what they had originally thought. I include statements on the organizer that may be presented in the illustrations. For example, in the organizer in Figure 5.2, the answer to the statement "Egypt is in Africa" can be found on a map on the website and is not included in the body of the text. The section titled "Other facts I found out" gives children the opportunity to record interesting information not mentioned on the organizer. Before preparing these organizers, read through the information on the website to locate the specific facts you want the children to locate.

Using the RAN

In Chapter 2 and in my book *Reality Checks: Teaching Reading Comprehension with Nonfiction* (2006b), I discuss the Reading and Analyzing Nonfiction strategy, or RAN, as an means for effectively assisting children as they gather new information. A RAN organizer is also a wonderful tool to help children read to gain specific information when researching on the computer. The RAN encourages children to read actively either to confirm or to negate prior thinking while gathering new information. Furthermore, RAN encourages learners to raise questions from the new facts found and to seek out other websites for answers. There are five categories in the RAN, which are explained next. Figure 5.3 shows an example of a fourth-grade student's RAN used to research polar bears. See Appendix N.

Name Anna Markell	Topic POLAR BEARS			Website/s seaworld.org/infbooks/polarbears/home/html. polarbearsinternational.org/bear-facts/	

Content	What I think I Know	C	M	New Facts	Wonderings
FOOD/ DIET	Seals Penguins People	✓	✓	Ringed Seals. They are in the antarctic Only when they are really hungry Eat dead whales	How many people do they kill? Answer Not many 1-2 each year
APPEARANCE	white weigh alot big paws thick fur	✓ ✓ ✓ ✓		largest land predator to keep warm. Weigh 330 to 550 pounds	Why are they white? Answer To sneak up on prey O
HABITAT	live in the snow	✓		On sea ice and on land in 5 nations U.S, Canada, Russia, Greenway, Norway Churchill is the polar bear capital.	

KEY : C—Confirmed information   M—Misconceptions   O—Other websites

Figure 5.3

Anna's RAN Organizer on Polar Bears

What I Think I Know

In this category, students state information they think to be correct about the topic they are researching. They will require demonstrations on how to keep their prior knowledge specific to the topic they are investigating. As seen in Figure 5.3, the topic was about polar bears, specifically their diet, appearance, and habitat. Anna was encouraged to record her background knowledge about these three categories rather than general information about polar bears.

In Noel Sorrento's fifth-grade classroom, the children were studying the American War of Independence. Noel found that by using categories dealing with time lines he was able to key his students into locating the specific information that he wanted them to acquire. He used the following three categories on the RAN: "Events leading up to the war," "What happened during the war," and "What happened after the war." In this way, the children were not simply recording and researching global information about the War of Independence but were gathering relevant information to the unit of study. This ensured that his students were focused when reading identified websites.

Confirmed

After recording prior knowledge, students read the identified websites to see whether they could confirm any of this information. As seen in Figure 5.3, Anna put a checkmark next to the statements she confirmed while viewing the websites as well as recorded extra details in the "New Facts" column.

Misconceptions

Apart from identifying confirmed prior knowledge, students are encouraged to also locate incorrect prior thinking as they read the websites. As seen in Figure 5.3, Anna indicated that polar bears do not eat penguins as she originally thought by placing a checkmark in the misconceptions column. She has also added the reason polar bears do not consume penguins in the "New Facts" column.

New Facts

In this category, students research to locate additional information not stated in their prior knowledge. As with the recording of information under the category "What I think I Know," students will require demonstration on how to only record new facts specific to the topic they are researching. As seen in Figure 5.3, Anna has included many new facts about the diet, appearance, and habitat of polar bears.

Wonderings

The inclusion of wonderings encourages children to raise questions based on the new information. To answer the questions they've raised, they can look at other websites apart from those bookmarked by the teacher. As seen in Figure 5.3, Anna has raised the question, "How many people are killed be polar bears?" This question was sparked by a fact she had read that stated polar bears will consume humans if they are really hungry. Anna looked for other websites to answer her question and found that only one or two people are killed by polar bear each year. She indicated that she got this information from another website by placing a letter O next to the answer to the question. Anna had done likewise with the answer to "Why are polar bears white?"

The K/1 Factor

When using the RAN with kindergarten and first-grade children, it is best to first limit the organizer to the first three categories. As seen in Figure 5.4, Zachary has drawn what he thinks he knows about frogs and Michelle Gaul, his kindergarten teacher, has recorded his thoughts underneath each picture. Zachary has then looked at a specific website on frogs and placed checkmarks on top of his illustrations to signify his prior thinking was correct. Zachary has then added drawings to represent new facts learned. Refer to Appendix O.

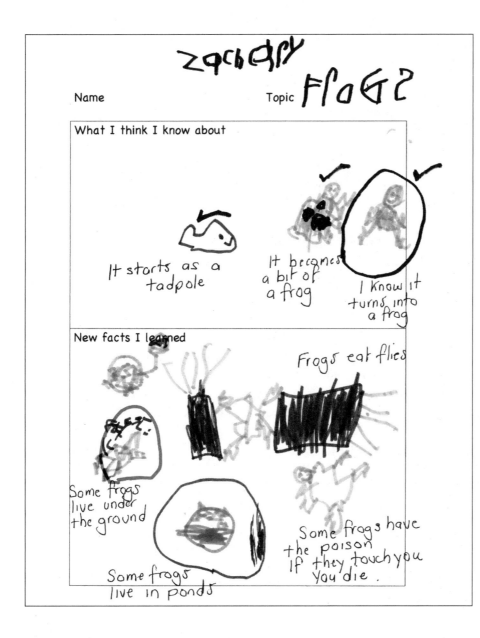

Figure 5.4
Zachary's RAN Organizer

Useful Websites for Independent Reading and Research

A list of useful and appropriate websites for children in primary and elementary grades follows. These have been organized under science and social studies topics that many schools have adapted as part of their curriculum.

   Note: At the time of publication, these websites were excellent sites for children to research on a specific topic. Given the changing nature of websites in terms of complexity and content, I recommend that the teacher view these sites before giving students independent access.

Science

Animals

http://www.kidscom.com/games/animal/animal.html
http://kidsgowild.com/
http://www.kbears.com/ (farm)
http://kids.nationalgeographic.com/
http://www.kidsbiology.com/animals-for-children.php
http://www.tropical-forests.com/ (rain forests)
http://www.junglemouse.net/ani/animals.html (rain forests)
http://www.nationalgeographic.com/features/00/earthpulse/
   rainforest/index_flash-feature.html (rain forests)
http://www.webtots.co.uk/ (for younger kids, farm)
http://www.ncmoa.org/costarica/ (rain forest/frogs)
http://nationalzoo.si.edu/Audiences/kids/

Space

http://www.nasa.gov/audience/forkids/kidsclub/flash/index.html
http://spaceplace.jpl.nasa.gov/en/kids/
http://www.seasky.org/
http://science.nationalgeographic.com/science/space/solar-system
http://www.nasa.gov/audience/forstudents/k-4/stories/what-is-the-
   solar-system.html
http://www.nineplanets.org
http://www.kidsastronomy.com/
http://www.kidskonnect.com/content/view/101/27/

The Ocean

http://www.seasky.org/
http://www.calstatela.edu/faculty/eviau/edit557/oceans/linda/loceans.
   htm

http://www.prekinders.com/ocean_kids.htm
http://sln.fi.edu/fellows/fellow8/dec98/intera.html
http://funschool.kaboose.com/globe-rider/under-the-sea/
http://www.didyouknow.org/kids/ocean.htm
http://kids.nationalgeographic.com/Animals/
http://www.seaworld.org/wild-world/safari/virtual-aquarium/
    acropora-coral.htm
http://www.kidzone.ws/sharks/index.htm

Plants and Trees

http://www.dnr.state.wi.us/org/caer/ce/eek/veg/trees/treestruecolor.
    htm
http://www.forgefx.com/casestudies/prenticehall/ph/solar_system/
    solarsystem.htm
http://www.urbanext.uiuc.edu/firstgarden/planning/index.html
http://www.primarygames.com/science/flowers/flowers.htm
http://sophia.smith.edu/badseeds/plantfacts.html
http://www.edenproject.com/childrens/1226.html
http://www.urbanext.uiuc.edu/kids/index.html
http://www.mbgnet.net/

Dinosaurs

http://www.sdnhm.org/kids/dinosaur/index.html
http://www.cotf.edu/ete/modules/msese/dinosaurflr/diorama.html
http://www.mantyweb.com/dinosaur/dinosaur_games.htm
http://www.fieldmuseum.org/sue/index.html
http://www.kidsdinos.com/
http://kids.nationalgeographic.com/Games/PuzzlesQuizzes/
    Brainteaserdinosaurs
http://easyweb.easynet.co.uk/~skafi/DINO.HTM

Reptiles and Frogs

http://nationalzoo.si.edu/Animals/ReptilesAmphibians/ForKids/
    default.cfm
http://www.kiddyhouse.com/Themes/frogs/
http://www.chevroncars.com/learn/wondrous-world/crocodile-facts
http://www.worldbook.com/wb/Students?content_spotlight/reptiles/
    facts

Birds

http://www.enchantedlearning.com/subjects/birds/
http://www.mbr-pwrc.usgs.gov/Infocenter/infocenter.html#Corvidae
http://www.atozkidsstuff.com/baldeagle.html (bald eagle)

http://www.kidsplanet.org/factsheets/bald_eagle.html (bald eagle)
http://www.birds.cornell.edu/schoolyard/all_about_birds/fun_with_
    birds/cool_facts.html
http://www.iwrc-online.org/kids/Facts/Birds/birds.htm
http://www.kidzone.ws/animals/birds2.htm (birds of prey)

Bugs/Creepy Crawlies
http://www.cdli.ca/CITE/creepy_crawlies.htm
http://coolbugstuff.com/facts.php?osCsid=ab1f1c8ce3ff9f6124512071
    9192801b
http://www.burgepest.com/bugfacts.htm
http://www.ex.ac.uk/bugclub
http://www.insects.org
http://www.ento.csiro.au/about_insects/index.html
http://www.insectfarm.com.au

Human Body/Nutrition
www.yuckydiscovery.com
http://www.brainpop.com/health
http://www.kidshealth.org/kid/
http://www.innerbody.com
http://vilenski.org/science/humanbody/
http://dir.yahoo.com/Health/

Weather
http://skydiary.com/kids/
http://www.scholastic.com/kids/weather/
http://www.weatherwizkids.com/
http://eo.ucar.edu/webweather/
http://www.tornadochaser.com/2000projects.htm
http://eo.ucar.edu/rainbows/
http://www.wxdude.com/

Energy
http://www.energyhog.org/childrens.htm
http://www.eere.energy.gov/kids/games.html
http://www.eia.doe.gov/kids/
http://www.eia.doe.gov/kids/energyfacts/sources/non-
    renewable/moreoil.html
http://www.nicor.com/en_us/nicor_inc/nicor_in_the_community/
    kid_sites.htm
http://www.energystar.gov/index.cfm?c=kids.kids_index
http://www.hightechkids.org/

Matter

http://www.chem4kids.com/files/matter_intro.html

http://kids.aol.com/HomeworkHelp/junior/science/matter

http://www2.mcdaniel.edu/Graduate/TI/pages/LEWIS/matterweb.
htm

http://www.idahoptv.org/dialogue4kids/season7/matter/facts.cfm

Rock and Minerals

Motion/Simple Machines

Social Studies

Countries

http://cyberschoolbus.un.org/infonation/index.asp

http://www.countryreports.org/

http://www.studentsoftheworld.info/menu_infopays.html

http://www.cantonpl.org/kids/country.html

http://www.dltk-kids.com/world/index.htm

http://kids.yahoo.com/directory/Around-the-World/Countries

http://northvalley.net/kids/cities.shtml

http://www.timeforkids.com/TFK/hh/goplaces/

http://kids.nationalgeographic.com/Games/GeographyGames/Geospy

Holidays/Celebrations

http://www.billybear4kids.com/

http://falcon.jmu.edu/~ramseyil/holidays.htm

http://www.suelebeau.com/months.htm

http://www.texaseducator.com/teacher/holidays.html

Transportation

http://www.chevroncars.com/learn/cars/car-fun-facts

http://www.spokanecleanair.org/cool_car_facts.asp

http://www.trakkies.co.uk/railway-facts/fun-facts

http://library.thinkquest.org/J001198/train.htm

http://www.gocitybus.com/kids/mainpage.htm

http://www.boeing.com/commercial/747family/pf/pf_facts.html

Recycling

www.howstuffworks.com

http://www.zerowaste.co.nz

http://www.nationalgeographic.com

http://www.envirolink.org

United States Geography

Presidents/Elections/The Whitehouse
http://www.kids.gov/
http://millercenter.org/academic/americanpresident/
http://www.whitehouse.gov/history/presidents/
http://memory.loc.gov/ammem/odmdhtml/preshome.html
http://score.rims.k12.ca.us/activity/presidentsday/
http://www.americanpresidents.org/
http://www.kidsolr.com/history/
http://www.whitehouse.gov/history/life/video/index.html

American Explorers
http://www.kidinfo.com/American_History/Explorers.html
http://www.lucidcafe.com/library/95aug/lewis.html
http://www.multcolib.org/homework/alphaexp.html
http://www.42explore2.com/explorers.htm
http://gardenofpraise.com/leaders.htm
http://www.eduweb.com/portfolio/jeffwest/index.html
http://www.nationalgeographic.com/west/index.html

Revolutionary War
http://memory.loc.gov/ammem/browse/ListSome.php?category=
    War,+Military
http://www.historyplace.com/unitedstates/revolution/index.html
http://www.historyplace.com/index.html
http://www.congressforkids.net/Independence_declaration_1.htm
http://www.kathimitchell.com/revolt.htm
http://www.kidskonnect.com/content/view/251/27/
http://www.pocanticohills.org/revolution/revolution.htm

Civil War
http://memory.loc.gov/ammem/browse/ListSome.php?category=War,
    +Military
http://www.historynet.com/magazines/americas_civil_war
http://www.historyplace.com/index.html
http://cybersleuthkids.com/sleuth/History/US_History/Civil_War/
    index.htm
http://www.pocanticohills.org/civilwar/cwar.htm
http://www.nps.gov/archive/gett/gettkidz/kidzindex.htm
http://www.kathimitchell.com/civil.htm

Good Choice!

Native Americans

http://www.carnegiemnh.org/exhibits/north-south-east-west/
    iroquois/index.html
http://www.ahsd25.k12.il.us/Curriculum%20Info/nativeamericans/
http://nativetech.org/games/index.php
http://www.native-languages.org/kids.htm
http://www.native-languages.org/kidfaq.htm

General

http://www.hightechscience.org/funfacts.htm
http://www.sciencekids.co.nz/sciencefacts.html
http://www.ask.com
http://www.enchantedlearning.com
http://www.classbrain.com
http://www.cia.gov/cia/publications/factbook/index.html
http://www.askforkids.com
http://www.education-world.com
http://www.kidsconnect.com/
http://www.education-world.com/
http://www.kidsinfo.com/

PART 3

Providing Support

Whole-Class Mini-Lessons in Selecting Texts and Reading Widely

E ven with a well-organized, inviting, and diverse classroom library, as discussed in Chapters 3 and 4, many children find it difficult to self-select appropriate materials for independent reading. When I first established independent reading time in my first-grade classroom, most of my children would select books based only on the cover. They would skim through their materials in record speed looking only at the pictures. They had few strategies for making informed selections when it came to using print to make meaning. When I taught fifth and sixth grades, many of my learners also struggled with the selection process. They too used the cover as their prime strategy for making selections. Consequently, they often chose materials that were too complex, thus compromising their comprehension. I also found that many of my students were not reading widely. They had become trapped in reading within a narrow field of topics and genres.

Whether I was teaching kindergarten or sixth grade, I needed to provide support for my learners in making wise selections through whole-class mini-lessons. These mini-lessons needed to be ongoing and concentrate on two major aspects of the selection process. First, the children needed to know how to select materials in which they were able to gain meaning from print as well as pictures. Second, they needed to choose materials that would broaden their reading repertoire and include a variety of topics and genres. Figure 6.1 gives an overview of some of the whole-class mini-lessons that I needed to provide based on these two aspects.

Figure 6.1
Overview of Possible Whole-Class Mini-Lessons

Mini-Lessons in Selecting Appropriate Texts	Mini-Lessons in Reading Widely
■ Understanding the terminology texts ■ Understanding the terms *comfortable* and *just right* ■ Identifying materials that are suitable selections such as read-alouds, texts introduced in shared and guided reading, books on tape, and materials previously read ■ Knowing when materials are too difficult ■ Being able to understand what you are reading ■ Using the blurb to determine suitability ■ Skimming through a text to determine suitability ■ Using color codes. (Refer to Chapter 8 for detailed information on color coding.) ■ Gaining information from visual sources such as pictures, diagrams, charts, maps, and labels ■ Strategizing to work out unknown words ■ Preparing for individual conferences (Refer to Chapter 7 for detailed information.)	■ Selecting texts based on personal interests ■ Selecting peer-recommended texts ■ Selecting texts based on units of study being implemented in the classroom ■ Reading a variety of topics when selecting nonfiction texts ■ Reading different genres when selecting fiction. For example, fantasy, fable, myths and legends, mysteries, adventures, realistic fiction, science fiction, and poetry ■ Reading different genres when selecting nonfiction. For example, explanations, procedures, persuasions, descriptions, and poetry ■ Selecting different forms of reading materials such as magazines, articles, newspapers, brochures, pamphlets, and flyers

Selecting Appropriate Texts Grades K–2

In Janet Mullins's first- and second-grade multiage classroom in a school in Melbourne, Australia, we initiated discussions on appropriate texts by bringing the children together and asking them how they knew when a text felt comfortable or just right. We refrained from using the terminology *just right books* because we wanted our learners to understand that reading is not just using books. We told them that the word *text* meant anything you read, and discussed how these could be books, magazines, newspapers, maps, cards, and other nonbook sources. We also discussed the meaning of the words *just right* and *comfortable*. We cannot assume that young learners understand our terminology no matter how simple it may appear to us. This raises the value of adopting a consistent school-wide vocabulary so that learners do not become confused by each teacher's personal terminology.

In Katie Benson's kindergarten classroom, we used the story of the three bears to explain "just right." We discussed baby bear's porridge to demonstrate the meaning of the word *just right*. We discussed with the children how Goldilocks found the mama bear's porridge too cold and the papa bear's porridge too hot but baby bear's porridge was just right. Similarly, we discussed the three bears' chairs and beds so that the children understood the notion of what comfortable or just right really meant. Steph Koch, a first-grade teacher from Twin Valley, Pennsylvania, used shoes and clothing to help her children understand the concept of comfortable or just right. Steph explained that just like shoes and clothes, reading materials can be uncomfortable and that they need to select texts that had a just right fit.

After discussing the words *just right* and *comfortable* with Janet's children, we charted their thinking on what helped them select materials that felt just right. We found their responses were varied but displayed a basic understanding of the selection process. It was evident that they had had these conversations with their teacher from the previous year. The chart Janet and I constructed with the children was placed in a prominent location in the classroom library, and we constantly encouraged them to refer to it when making selections. We also added to the chart as we discovered new strategies for making selections.

How We Know When a Text Is Comfortable and Just Right

- You can read it.
- It is something you want to read.
- You understand most of the words.
- It's something you have heard before.
- It's something you have read before.

- The words are easy to read.
- You can tell the story from the pictures.
- It's something you can listen to on a tape or CD.

We provided the children with many whole-class mini-lessons on the different strategies highlighted on the chart. For instance, for the strategy "It's something you've heard before," we made them aware that previously introduced materials in read-aloud and shared and guided reading encounters were examples of such texts. We showed them where to locate these materials in the classroom library and encouraged them to make these part of their selections. Janet had many books on tape so one of our mini-lessons centered on how these were appropriate selections and could be borrowed. Although some of these texts were at readability levels above many of the children's independent reading levels, the extra support from the oral retelling made them appropriate. We found that books on tapes were particularly supportive for our English as a second language learners.

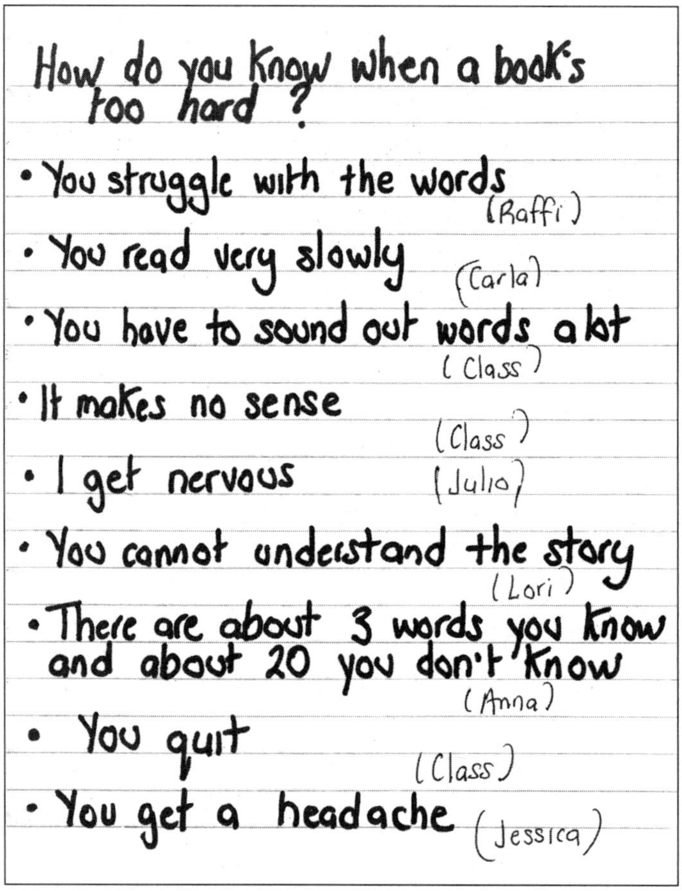

Although Janet and I provided many whole-class mini-lessons on when a text felt comfortable, many children using these strategies were not always successful. It appeared they were able to articulate the strategies but were not always able to put their thinking into practice. We decided to take a different tack. In addition to discussing when a text feels right, we also talked about when a text feels wrong, as seen in Figure 6.2. This proved to be a highly successful strategy and provided additional assistance to our learners in the selection process. The conversations with the children were far richer when we discussed when they felt something was too hard than when we discussed what was just right, partly because strong feelings are evoked when something doesn't feel quite right. It is more tangible for young readers.

Figure 6.2
Chart Showing When We Know a Book Is Too Hard

How do you know when a book's too hard?

- You struggle with the words (Raffi)
- You read very slowly (Carla)
- You have to sound out words a lot (Class)
- It makes no sense (Class)
- I get nervous (Julia)
- You cannot understand the story (Lori)
- There are about 3 words you know and about 20 you don't know (Anna)
- You quit (Class)
- You get a headache (Jessica)

Strategies for Working Out Unknown Words

The conversations on when a text felt uncomfortable opened up further discussions, namely, what to do when you come across a word you can't read or understand. We were finding that some of the children were discarding their selected texts because they were encountering a handful of unknown words and therefore deemed it an uncomfortable read. It appeared that while Janet and I had discouraged many of the children from selecting texts that were too hard, we needed to clarify that just because there may be a few words you don't know, this doesn't necessarily mean the text is too complex. We wanted them to understand that it is only when there are many unknown words that the text can be deemed too difficult. Through ongoing whole-class conversations and demonstrations, we constructed a chart with the children to help them use strategies to figure out unknown words. See Figure 6.3. We discussed with the children both what to do when they can't say the word and what to do when they don't know the meaning of the word. Many of the children were challenged by having to decode certain words as well as by the meanings of words. We didn't want them to use their word strategies to decode challenging vocabulary and then continue reading even when meaning was being compromised.

Figure 6.3
Chart Showing What to Do If You Don't Know the Meaning of a Word

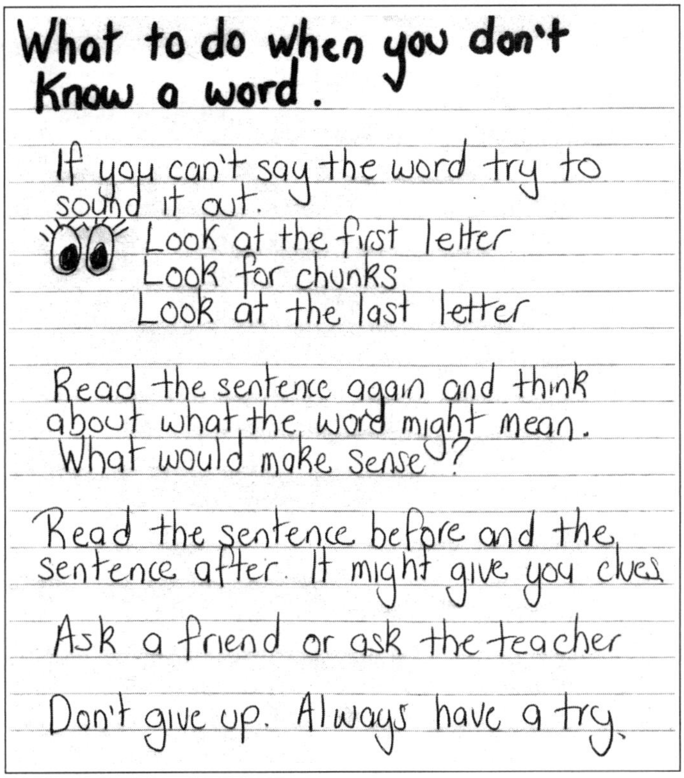

What to do when you don't know a word.

If you can't say the word try to sound it out.
Look at the first letter
Look for chunks
Look at the last letter

Read the sentence again and think about what the word might mean. What would make sense?

Read the sentence before and the sentence after. It might give you clues

Ask a friend or ask the teacher

Don't give up. Always have a try.

Understanding What You Are Reading

The most important understanding that Janet and I wanted the children to acquire in text selection was that it had to be something they could comprehend. Through ongoing read-aloud, shared reading, and guided reading encounters, we explored many specific comprehension strategies. See Figure 6.4. Note: More information on how to specifically teach these strategies can be found in *Reality Checks: Teaching*

Key Strategies

Literal Understandings	Interpretive Understandings	Evaluative Understandings
Strategies that require the student to recall or recognize plots, settings, characters, ideas, and facts that are explicitly stated	Strategies that require the student to use the literal information presented in the text to make connections and inferences based on background knowledge and personal experiences	Strategies that require the student to use literal and interpretive understandings to make judgments as to the content of what he or she is reading

Specific Strategies

■ Retelling
■ Visualizing
■ Sequence of events or instructions
■ Summarizing
■ Locating specific information and using specific text features such as a table of contents, headings, and index to achieve this
■ Finding supportive details
■ Gaining information from visual sources
■ Cause and effect
■ Problem/solution
■ Compare and contrast
■ Main idea/s
	■ Predicting and Inferring:
	  what will happen
	  cause and effect
	  problem/solution
	  main idea/s
	  sequences/events
	  comparisons
	  information from visual
	    sources
	■ Making Connections
	  text to self
	  text to text
	  text to world
	■ Visualizing
		■ Synthesize information
		■ Visualizing
		■ Fact versus opinion
		■ Reality versus fantasy
		■ Validity of a piece
		■ Adequacy of a piece
		■ Relevance of a piece
		■ Author bias
		■ Author intent
		■ Point of view
		■ Tools/craft used by the author to affect thinking
		■ Making overall judgments on a piece

Figure 6.4
Key Comprehension
Strategies

Reading Comprehension with Nonfiction (Stead 2006b). Publications by Allen (2000), Harvey and Goudis (2007), Hoyt (2005), Keene and Zimmermann (2007), and Miller (2002) also contain valuable strategies for developing comprehension.

We impressed on the children that when making selections to always remember that reading was more than getting through the words. Regardless of whether it was a piece of fiction or nonfiction, a newspaper or a magazine, we wanted the children to go beyond just retelling what they had read. We wanted them to question, to connect with, to infer from, and to evaluate what they were reading.

Gaining Information from Visual Sources

Most materials at early readability levels contain supporting pictures to match the text. Indeed, for pre-emergent readers, pictures are their prime source for constructing meaning. With Janet's first- and second-grade children, we had many conversations about how you can use these pictures to make sense of a book even when you can't read all the words. We modeled for them how you can tell a story using primarily the pictures but encouraged them to also select materials they could actually read. Unless they were pre-emergent readers, we didn't want them to rely solely on illustrations for meaning.

With respect to nonfiction materials, we stressed the importance of gaining new information from the illustrations. Unlike fiction illustrations, where the pictures visualize what is being said in the text, nonfiction illustrations can supply additional information. Children need demonstrations on how to read these illustrations to gain additional understandings. Janet and I read the following information about a shark from *The Great White Shark* by James Hirsch.

> *Great white sharks are predators. This means they hunt other creatures. They eat smaller or weaker animals but no animal eats them.*

We showed them the accompanying photograph. See Figure 6.5. We then asked the children to tell us all the information that the picture told us that wasn't in the text. Here are their responses:

Figure 6.5
Picture of a Shark

Information from the Picture

Sharks have lots of teeth.
Sharks have a big mouth.
Sharks' teeth are very pointy.
Sharks like to eat seals.
Sharks close their eyes when they attack.
Sharks have a pointy nose.
Some of the sharks' teeth are longer than others.

This mini-lesson was a valuable means of showing the children that when selecting nonfiction texts, regardless of whether you can read the words, you can get lots of new information from the pictures. As with their fiction selections, we stressed the importance of also selecting materials they could actually read, not just material for which they were using the illustrations to gather information.

Selecting Appropriate Texts Grades 3–6

By third grade, it is hoped that most students are able to select appropriate texts for independent reading; however, this is not always the case. Depending on discussions and demonstrations in previous years, I often find that students in grades three through six struggle with the selection process much like their younger counterparts. These students also require ongoing demonstrations in selecting materials.

I begin the school year by asking the students to write down how they know when a text is suitable, as seen in Figure 6.6. A form that you may wish to use can be found in Appendix P.

In essence, this is a preassessment of each child's understanding of the selection process. Too often older learners shut down in whole-class discussions, unlike the children in earlier grades, who constantly want their opinions heard. This is also true for English as a second language learners, who often lack the confidence to speak up in front of their peers. Having students record their thinking independently acts as a springboard for healthy whole-class discussions so that all learners will have something to share.

Once completed, I bring the students together to share their strategies. I also share with them strategies I use. I type up a master list and distribute it to each student. See Figure 6.7. Students put this list into their reading binders. Refer to Chapter 7 for information about establishing reading binders. By receiving a copy of the list, each child can refer to it when selecting materials from the classroom library and from

Figure 6.6
Tehanee's List of Strategies for Selecting a Suitable Text

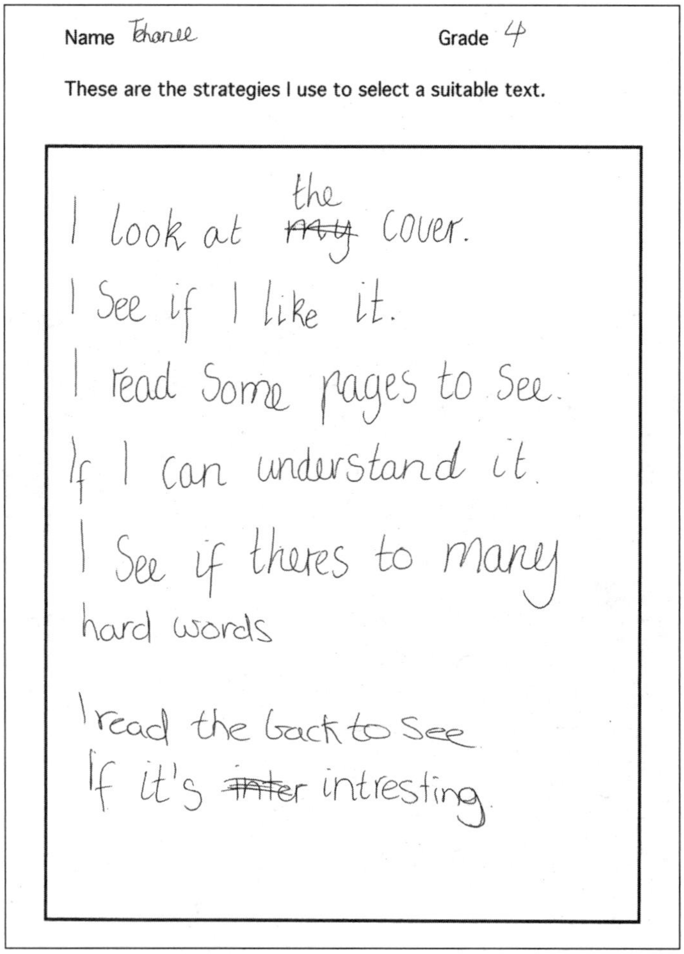

Name Tehanee   Grade 4

These are the strategies I use to select a suitable text.

I look at the ~~my~~ cover.
I see if I like it.
I read some pages to see.
If I can understand it.
I see if theres to many hard words

I read the back to see
If it's ~~inter~~ intresting.

Figure 6.7

Chart Showing
Strategies for Selecting
Suitable Texts

Strategies for Selecting Suitable Texts

Read the first few pages. If you can understand what's happening, then it's probably suitable.

Read the blurb. If you can read and understand it, then it may be suitable.

Skim through the text. If you see lots of words you can't say or you don't know the meaning of, then it might be too difficult.

If it's a nonfiction piece, you may be able to get information from the illustrations. This makes it suitable but make sure you also have selections where you *can* read and understand the print.

If it's part of a series and you've read other titles, then it is probably suitable.

It's okay to have materials that are easy reads or materials you have read before and want to revisit, but also include materials that might be a little more challenging.

There may be a color code on the back of the book to help you.

the school and local public library. As students discover more strategies to help with the selection process, they add them to their lists.

As seen in Figure 6.7, there are many focuses for whole-class discussions on selecting suitable texts, and it is necessary to have continual conversations with the students during the school year to help them understand and apply these strategies. Because students are able to articulate these strategies in the first mini-lesson doesn't mean they have fully understood and internalized them. Note: The color-coding strategy at the bottom of Figure 6.7 will be discussed in detail in Chapter 8.

One focus for whole-class mini-lessons is that a suitable text can be something that is well within your comfort zone. There is nothing wrong with reading a favorite book a second time. I certainly love rereading a novel I've read in the past. I sometimes enjoy it more on the second read. Rereading a known text is also relevant for nonfiction. Information about a topic of high interest can be read many times to deepen and connect with content understandings. For example, when my son went away to camp, he asked me to care for his lizard. He gave me a small booklet and told me that it contained the basics on feeding and caring for his pet. I must have read that booklet twenty times. The rereads were not only to help me care for his scaly friend. I became fascinated by these creatures and found that each time I reread a section I gained deeper understandings about lizards. Nonfiction materials can contain lots of information, and sometimes you need to revisit a text to connect with what you may have missed on the first read. Also, students may not need to read all of their nonfiction selections. They may just want to read selected chapters.

Strategies for Working Out Unknown Words

As with children in earlier grades, conversations about what to do when you encounter unknown words is important in helping older students with the selection process. For fluent readers, the challenge is not decoding texts but comprehending texts. If students are not gaining meaning from what they are reading, regardless of their ability to decode the words, then the text is probably too difficult.

Furthermore, students need to understand that a small percentage of unknown words doesn't equate to a difficult text. In Peter Miller's fifth-grade classroom, we brought his students together to discuss strategies for dealing with unknown words. We constructed a chart and divided the strategies into two major categories, primary and secondary. See Figure 6.8. These categories were based on work I had done with Lisa Moynihan in her third-grade class in New York and are documented in more detail in *Reality Checks: Teaching Reading Comprehension with Nonfiction* (2006b).

Primary strategies are those where the student uses techniques within the body of the text to solve word meanings. Secondary strate-

Figure 6.8
Strategies for Understanding the Meanings of Unknown Words

Finding the Meanings of Unknown Words

Primary Strategies
- Look for context clues.
  - Read it over and put in a word that would make sense.
  - Reread the sentences before.
  - Read the sentence after.
  - Look for important words around it.
- Break the word apart and think about the meaning of each part.
- Use any illustrations that might help.

Secondary Strategies
- Look in the glossary.
- Look in a dictionary.
- Ask a friend.
- Ask the teacher.

Good Choice!

gies require the student to go outside the body of the text whether it be a glossary at the back of the book, a dictionary, or simply asking another person for assistance. Our goal was to encourage Peter's students to use primary strategies before secondary strategies. We didn't want them always going outside the body of the text to find word meanings as this inevitably interrupts the reading and can compromise comprehension.

Understanding What You Are Reading

As with younger children, students in grades three through six need ongoing learning experiences in making meaning through read-aloud and shared and guided reading encounters, which will assist them in making wiser decisions when selecting suitable texts for independent reading. The specific strategies shown in Figure 6.4 will shape learning experiences students need to deepen their reading comprehension. The second edition of *Strategies That Work* by Harvey and Goudvis (2007) is a particularly beneficial resource when working with students in grades three through six to help them deepen comprehension.

Gaining Information from Visual Sources

As with children in earlier grades, have discussions with fluent readers in a whole-class setting about the importance of visual information in nonfiction. With fiction, especially novels, students need to be able to read the text to gain understandings of plot and characters, but this is not always necessary in nonfiction. Students can easily access a wealth of information using only visual sources.

Peter's students were studying a unit on space. We had gathered many books and magazines about the topic but found that some of these texts were complex and above most students' independent reading level. We held discussions with the students and showed them that if they could access information from the illustrations, even if the written text was too complex, then the text was a suitable choice for independent reading. Peter and I had found that many of his students discarded nonfiction material they deemed too complex. They hadn't considered that if meaning could be gained from the illustrations, then the text was a suitable choice. Although I encouraged Peter's students to include these texts in their selections, I also impressed on them the importance of having texts they could read. I didn't want their acquisition of reading vocabulary halted because of an overreliance on visual elements.

It really is a question of balance. Although I never want to restrict students' choices of reading materials, I do need to encourage them to select a majority of materials at appropriate independent reading levels. An exclusive diet of "easy" reading materials or only gathering information from visual sources in materials that are too hard will do little to foster and extend reading growth.

Broadening the Reading Diet

We want children to select texts that they can read and understand; however, we also want them to read widely. We want them to understand that there are different kinds of reading in their lives. Whole-class mini-lessons should lead children to understand the need for a combination of different kinds of reading. Some selections will be based on personal interest; others will include teacher-recommended texts such as materials introduced in read-aloud and shared and guided reading encounters. Others will be part of research projects stemming from science and social studies units. Some may be texts suggested by their classmates. As with demonstrations in selecting suitable texts, these whole-class mini-lessons need to occur throughout the year. Refer to Figure 6.1 for an overview of mini-lessons on reading widely.

Charts created from discussions stemming from these mini-lessons should be revisited throughout the school year. We cannot assume that children will internalize learning with one discussion or demonstration.

Reading Widely Grades K–2

In Janet's first-grade classroom, we opened discussions with her students about reading widely by asking them what they thought were good choices when making selections. We recorded these on a chart. Janet and I added our own recommendations to this chart to broaden children's understandings of the variety of texts they could borrow.

What Are Good Choices?
A favorite read-aloud
A favorite shared reading book
Stories I want to read
Magazines I want to read
Nonfiction that interests me
A book I've had in guided reading
My current guided reading book

A book about the topic we are exploring
Books that friends have told me are good to read
Books that are recommended by my teacher

Peer-Recommended Texts

We provided many demonstrations based on the chart we had constructed, including how students can recommend favorite materials to their peers. We asked them to write down the titles of texts they liked and would recommend to their friends. This proved challenging because the children wanted to record every book they had read. We clarified that they needed to select only their favorite texts. To help them accomplish this, we asked them to record only four books they really liked and then circle their two favorites. We then asked them to choose the one they thought was their favorite of the two. This strategy gave the children a tangible method for narrowing down their selection to an absolute favorite. We then set up a chart called "Our Favorite Things to Read" and recorded their selections. Many children selected texts similar to their favorite so we put a checkmark next to particular titles to indicate how many people had made it their first choice. As children found new favorite books and materials, we added these to the chart. We encouraged the children to look at this chart for suggested titles when selecting materials during independent reading.

Although students were eager to read texts suggested by their peers, the recommended material was not always at suitable readability levels. Our struggling readers often selected texts recommended by our fluent readers. This dilemma appeared to conflict with our belief system. On the one hand, we were asking our learners not to select texts that were too hard, but on the other hand, we were encouraging them to select materials recommended by their peers that could be in fact too complex. We realized that recommended difficult-to-read texts were fine as selections as long as someone read the text with them or to them. We revisited our strategy charts for selecting suitable texts, and when to know if a text is too hard. We asked the children to always remember that most of their selections needed to be a comfortable fit.

Texts Based on Content Studies

We also discussed how books on topics we were studying were wise choices. When Janet's students were studying animals as part of a science unit, she encouraged them to select material from the "Animals" basket. Although they were at liberty to select other nonfiction materials from other baskets, we wanted them to have at least one text about animals. This allowed for common talk around a central theme and strengthened specific content understandings. In helping them make selections, we limited one animal book or magazine per child because we were still building up our resources on animals and didn't have enough materials for the children to borrow multiple pieces. Naturally, they all wanted to borrow more than one text so we encouraged them to trade among themselves after they finished with a selected text. This proved to be a highly successful strategy. It enabled the materials to change hands at a faster rate.

Finding the Balance

Eventually, the children learned that there were three types of texts for independent reading: (1) materials they had chosen themselves based purely on interest or those recommended to them by their peers; (2) books introduced in guided reading; and (3) at least one piece of non-fiction that was connected with the science or social studies unit.

Our greatest challenge: our young learners wanted to read everything. They were like insatiable little bookworms. This is one of the delights of teaching children in kindergarten through grade two. They devour books, and their need to read widely is only limited by the expectations of the teacher. They will read virtually anything if it's been recommended. Janet and I decided that we needed to limit the number of texts they were borrowing to five or six. We implemented this limit after realizing that her students were borrowing twenty to thirty books at a time. Limiting selections ensured that they didn't become overwhelmed with too much material. It also guaranteed we had enough material left in the classroom library for everyone to borrow. The quality of the material, not the quantity, is important. We wanted them to take time and make wise decisions. Furthermore, we didn't want them racing through their reading materials in record speed. We wanted them to read, reread, and connect with their selections.

Reading Widely Grades 3–6

As with Janet's children, Peter Miller's fifth-grade students were at liberty to self-select materials based on their own interests. They too were encouraged to have at least one text based on a current unit of study.

When they studied the Revolutionary War, they were expected to select one piece of literature on this topic. Their independent reading also constituted either the text introduced in guided reading or a text introduced as part of a novel study or book club. We also encouraged them to recommend texts to one another and found that their reading logs were a perfect means to accomplish this goal. As discussed in Chapter 1, having each student keep a reading log that uses stars to rate how much they enjoyed reading the text gives them an avenue for making recommendations.

Extending Selections of Genres and Topics

One challenge Peter and I encountered was that his students were reading in a narrow field of fiction genres and a limited range of nonfiction topics. This is especially true—and natural—for many fluent readers in grades three through six. It is easy to be drawn to a series, books by a specific author, or materials on topics of interest that provide pleasurable reading. Unlike younger readers, who will attempt just about any topic, the more mature reader has already developed specific literary tastes. This is true for both fiction and nonfiction. Typically, with fiction, many boys seem to focus on mysteries, adventures, horror, and science fiction. Many girls also appear to enjoy adventure and mysteries but are also drawn to fairy tales, biographies, and, of course, by sixth and seventh grade, romance.

Contrary to popular belief with respect to nonfiction, there appear to be few borders between the interests of girls and boys. Individual taste prevails. Aside from topics about creepy crawlies, reptiles, and anything slimy, which many older girls still seem to be repelled by, most other topics are as satisfying for girls as they are for boys. Material revolving around space, animals, experiments, history, or other elements of our physical and social world seem largely based on individual preference regardless of gender. Although including nonfiction in classrooms over the past five years has provided more eclectic choices for our students, they still select materials in a limited range of topics, much like they select materials in a limited range of genres when reading fiction. Take Jason and Fiona, for example. Jason's reading diet consisted primarily of materials about reptiles, whereas Fiona selected only books about horses. Although Peter encouraged his students to peruse topics and genres of interest, he also wanted them to be open to other reading possibilities. I suggested that the catalyst for change would stem from providing diverse examples of literature through whole-class read-aloud encounters.

Read-Aloud Encounters

When Peter reflected on his read-aloud selections he was not surprised to find that 90 percent of his selections were novels. Like many teachers of grades three to six, he used a novel study as his anchor for the read-aloud encounter. Each day he read several chapters of a selected novel, and his students engaged in conversations about what had been read. Peter continued to read the entire novel over the course of two weeks and then selected a new novel to read aloud. Peter's students enjoyed this daily ritual, but he realized that he was doing little to diversify his learner's personal selections. He had given little thought to looking at the actual genre of the read-alouds he had selected. He made changes to his selection process and chose different types of novels to read to his students. He selected novels from a range of mysteries, adventures, realistic fiction, science fiction, fantasy, and fables.

Peter further realized he needed to include nonfiction materials as part of the read-aloud encounter and that these were not restricted to books: they could be magazines, newspaper articles, editorials, pamphlets, and brochures. This alteration constituted new thinking for Peter. He had never considered reading nonfiction to his children. Although he included nonfiction pieces in his shared and small-group instruction, he had never considered the power of reading aloud informational texts to his students that would spur them to select these texts in their own independent reading. Janet, in first grade, also had this realization. Typically, in kindergarten through second-grade classrooms, 95 percent of read-aloud encounters are stories.

After Peter completed reading a specific text type, he let students know that the classroom library had other examples of such texts for independent reading. After reading a mystery, he would inform his students that there were other mysteries available for selection in the mysteries basket in the classroom library. If the book was part of a series, he would inform his students where the other titles from the series were housed. Likewise, after reading aloud from a piece of nonfiction, Peter showed his students from which topic basket he had selected the text. Peter found that by making this simple link between the daily read-aloud and his students' independent reading, his learners began to vary their reading sections. Just as a child is attracted to the newest toy or game, so are they enticed to read materials that have been highlighted in a whole-class setting.

Should I Read the Entire Novel or Book?

Peter recognized that by always reading entire novels to his class he wasn't encouraging his students to read the selected texts for themselves. I suggested to Peter that he begin to alternate reading entire texts with reading partial texts. I proposed that after he had concluded reading an entire novel to the class he spend the next two weeks reading only a few chapters of selected novels and then letting his students know that the book was available for independent reading. Peter was amazed at the impact this had on his students. It was as if he had ignited a fire. The partial reading of a book had hooked his learners. They wanted to know how the stories ended, so everyone wanted to read the selected text. Because we only had limited copies of specific novels, we read the first few chapters of selected novels over the course of two weeks, and at the end of this period, learners could sign up to read the novels they wanted to add to their reading repertoire. Peter stocked the classroom library with multiple copies of texts previewed in read-aloud encounters. The librarian became his best friend because the library housed multiple copies of specific novels. At times, Peter found that texts he had selected to read were boring for his learners. This led to healthy discussions about when it's acceptable to stop reading a book, a magazine, or an article.

Regarding nonfiction texts he read to the students, Peter realized that it was not always necessary to read entire books or articles. Sometimes he read selected chapters and then let his students know the text was available for borrowing.

Selecting Different Forms of Texts

I demonstrated to Peter how to entice his learners to select different forms of texts, not just books. I selected newspaper articles for this lesson because they had not been part of his students' selections even though a basket of articles was included in the classroom library. I selected a fascinating article from my local newspaper about a seventy-two-year-old dog owner who was mystified by the death of her sixteen-year-old pet. The dog had become seriously ill even though her local veterinarian had administered medication. Eventually, the owner had the dog put down to relieve its suffering. On the way back from the vet, the owner picked up photos she had recently taken that included two pictures of her beloved dog. In one of the photos, she had photographed a deadly tiger snake attacking her pet. While taking the photo the owner recalled seeing something flicker into the frame but had thought it was the camera strap. Incredibly, the owner had captured the precise moment at which the snake had delivered a fatal strike to her dog.

The children were spellbound by the story and the accompanying photograph, and they all wanted to read the article. I informed the students that I had made many copies of this article and others that I thought were fascinating and had placed them in the classroom library for independent reading. I suggested that students could cut out interesting newspaper articles and place them in scrapbooks for borrowing. Peter's students were enthusiastic. In the past, they had barely considered reading newspaper articles. Now they were including this medium as a valued part of their independent reading. Peter realized that just as I had implemented this lesson with newspaper articles, so too could he extend the types of texts selected by his students by modelling a variety of different forms of print such as brochures, pamphlets, flyers, and charts.

7

Establishing Individual Conferences to Support Children in Selecting Texts and Reading Widely

I n Chapter 6, we examined the importance of providing whole-class scaffolds to assist children in making wise selections for independent reading. Individual conferences provide additional support for monitoring these selections. In a conference, the teacher meets with individual students to discuss their reading and to make recommendations. It is not so much a time to teach new strategies but an opportunity to help students consolidate the strategies modeled in whole- and small-group settings.

Many teachers find conferences time-consuming, and I can certainly relate to that. At one time, I used conferences primarily for new teaching and would spend twenty to twenty-five minutes with each child, leaving scant time to conduct whole-class and small-group instruction. When I reflected on my practice, I realized I was repeating

Whole-Class Mini-Lessons	Individual Conferences	Small-Group Support
■ Introduce new strategies in selecting appropriate texts ■ Introduce new strategies for reading widely ■ Revisit and extend strategies previously taught	■ Monitor and solidify strategies in selecting appropriate texts ■ Monitor and solidify strategies for reading widely ■ Enable the teacher to access which strategies need to be revisited and extended in whole-class mini-lessons ■ Enable the teacher to access which strategies need to be revisited and extended in small-group settings	■ Based on observation from individual conferences, gives additional support for learners in selecting appropriate texts and reading widely

Figure 7.1

Overview of Providing Support in Selected Texts and Reading Widely

my instruction with different children who had similar needs. Sometimes I was saying the same things to just about every child. Clearly, this was an ineffective use of time. If most of my students had not internalized the strategies taught in the whole-class setting, then I needed to do another whole-class mini-lesson, rather than attempt to use the individual conference as the prime method for further instruction. If children with similar needs had not internalized whole-class mini-lessons, then I brought them together in small-group instruction rather than conferring with each student separately. This made my teaching life easier. Figure 7.1 gives a visual of this new thinking that now governs my teaching.

What to Look for in a Conference

Although this chapter is specifically focused on how the individual conference can be used to monitor and extend children's understanding in how to choose appropriate texts and read widely, the conference is also a powerful medium to monitor and extend many other reading strategies. *On Solid Ground* by Sharon Taberski (2000), *Beyond Leveled Books* by Karen Szymusiak, Franki Sibberson, and Lisa Koch (2008), *Growing Readers* by Kathy Collins (2004), and *Guiding Readers and Writers* by Irene Fountas and Gay Su Pinnell (2001) are excellent resources in how to use the conference to strengthen children's abilities as readers. The following is a list of some of the possible focuses for the reading conference:

- To formally and informally monitor and assess children's instructional reading level
- To give extra support to struggling readers in using reading strategies
- To promote a love of reading
- To observe each student's ability to:
  - Discuss information read
  - Gain literal, interpretive, and evaluative understandings (refer to Figure 6.4)
  - Include both fiction and nonfiction texts in their selections for independent reading
  - Select both fiction and nonfiction material at appropriate readability levels
  - Independently read materials for a substantive amount of time (reading stamina)
  - Read with fluency
  - Read with expression
  - Interpret information from illustrative sources such as pictures, tables, graphs, and maps
  - Use strategies to work out the meaning of unknown words
  - Read widely with fiction, for example, fantasy, fables, adventures, mysteries, science fiction, realistic fiction, and poetry
  - Read widely with nonfiction, for example, biographies, magazines, maps, articles, descriptions, scientific explanations, procedures, persuasions, and poetry

Setting Up Conferences

The amount of time to set aside for an individual conference varies according to the needs of each child. My goal is to keep conferences brief but focused. I aim for five to ten minutes per week per child. However, I allow more time for struggling readers, to provide an extra layer of support. Ideally, conferences should occur when the children are engaged in their daily twenty minutes of independent reading time, as outlined in Chapter 1; however, they can occur anytime throughout the day when you have a spare five minutes. The advantage of conducting conferences during independent reading time is that the rest of the classroom is quiet as children engage in their own reading. This allows for concentrated, uninterrupted time to meet with individual learners. In Peter Miller's fifth-grade classroom, some of his students arrived at school early, so we arranged to meet with them before the school day started. In Katie Benson's kindergarten class, the last half hour of the

Monday	Tuesday	Wednesday	Thursday	Friday
Jaydon	Jason	Betty S.	Selena	Jay
Marlena	Gerrard	Mark	Kathy	Amanda
Justin	Frankie	Jamie	Josie	Kirk
Sara	Betty R.	Franco	Brittany	Pete
Jessica	Crystal	Sally	Mina	Juan
			Gavin	
	Harold			

Figure 7.2
Conferencing Schedule

school day was for developmental play centers, so she used this time to meet with individual children.

The first step in organizing conferences is to establish a time for each child to meet with you during the week. In Melanie Jarrod's fourth-grade classroom in the Bronx, New York, we established the conferencing schedule shown in Figure 7.2. This schedule was placed in the classroom library where it could be seen by all the children so that they knew which day they were scheduled to meet with Melanie. The children's names were written on cards so they could be moved to different days in case Melanie needed to reorganize her weekly roster. For example, originally, Jason was scheduled to meet with Melanie every Monday, but because he received extra reading instruction by an interventional specialist, Melanie changed his conference day to Tuesday. If a child is absent on the day of his or her conference, that child's name is placed at the bottom of the chart to signify that the conference needs to be rescheduled. When a child is absent, Melanie meets with another child scheduled for the following day, and then she'll meet with the absent child when he or she returns to school. As seen in Figure 7.2, Harold was absent on Tuesday so his name was placed at the bottom of the chart to indicate that he had missed his scheduled conference. Melanie therefore met with Betty S., who was scheduled for Wednesday, and then she met with Harold on the following day.

The Reading Conference Express

When I worked with Lauren Benjamin in her first-grade classroom in New York, we established the reading conference express. I got this idea from a group of teachers I worked with at the Roosevelt School in Boston, Massachusetts. As seen in Figure 7.3, some of the teachers decided to establish reading trains in their classrooms to make independent reading a fun and engaging time. This stemmed from conversations they had with their children on where people read. Reading on a train was one of their responses so many of the teachers established these trains in their classrooms. Each day, four to five children boarded the train to read. The trains were numbered so that each class had its own uniquely numbered train. In one of the classrooms there was a conductor who wore a conductor's cap and gave out train tickets to passengers. I really must give kudos to these teachers for making reading a joyous occasion in their classrooms.

Lauren and I took this great idea and used it for conferencing with her students. Using a conferencing schedule similar to Figure 7.2, each day selected children boarded the Reading Conference Express to meet with Lauren. As seen in Figure 7.4, Lauren confers with Max. When she has finished her conversations with him, she will say, "Next Stop—Julia." At this point, Max will go to the end of the train and all the

Figure 7.3
The Reading Train

Figure 7.4
The Reading
Conference Express

children will slide one seat closer to Lauren. Therefore, Julia, who is second in line, will now move to the seat vacated by Max. It will be Julia's turn to conference with Lauren.

This proved to be a successful strategy because it ensured that all the children scheduled for a conference on a particular day were already together and ready to go. Lauren wasn't losing valuable time waiting for children to come to the conference when it was their turn.

In Peter's fifth-grade class, we also established a conferencing schedule, but the students met with Peter at the conferencing table. Peter used a table in the classroom and the students came to that table when it was their time for a conference. To save time in between conferences, Peter established a waiting chair just next to the conferencing table where the next student in line for a conference sat and prepared for his or her meeting with Peter.

Informal Conferencing

Many teachers find that it's simpler to walk around the room and informally provide support rather than set up formal conferences to monitor children's selections. This can be effective as long as adequate records are kept of each child's personal goals and the conference doesn't disturb the other children at the table. Even when a more formal approach to conferencing is used, as described in this chapter, informally walking around the room to give additional support is a useful strategy.

Students Preparing for Conferences

Children need to know what to expect at a conference and to come prepared. In Janet Mullins's first- and second-grade classroom, several whole-class mini-lessons centered on helping her students prepare for the conference. Together we constructed a chart, as seen in Figure 7.5. We kept the chart simple and asked the children to refer to it before they met with Janet. Making sure that the children were prepared ensured that the conferences were focused and implemented in a timely fashion. In kindergarten classrooms, it is advantageous to have small pictures or icons next to each point so that pre-emergent and beginning readers have an anchor for remembering each point.

In Peter's fifth-grade class, several of our whole-class mini-lessons also examined the importance of student preparation. The chart we constructed with his students can be seen in Figure 7.6. Peter's students were aware of the importance of being prepared. The day before their scheduled conference they were expected to go through each point on the chart—like a checklist—to ensure they were ready for the conference.

How to Get Ready for a Conference

- Make sure you know which day is your conference day. Look at the conference chart if you forget.
- Make sure you bring your book bag.
- Think about what you were supposed to work on in your reading. Ask the teacher if you forget.
- Have the book or text ready to share.

Figure 7.5
How to Get Ready for a Conference: K–2

How I Prepare for a Reading Conference

- I know what day I am scheduled for my conference.
- I come with appropriate materials (the texts I am reading, my reading binder, pen, pencil, etc.).
- I know what my goals are from the last conference.
- I have worked on these goals.
- I am ready to discuss these goals.
- I have any question that I need to ask written on sticky notes or in my reading binder.

Figure 7.6
How to Prepare for a Conference: 3–6

The Conference in Action

Once children know when they will be attending the conference and are prepared for the encounter, the conference can begin. The conference must be a focused event, so I follow a sequence of implementation procedures to help with this task. These procedures include the following:

Implementation Procedures

- I ask the student to tell me what he or she has been working on in independent reading. This is based on the tasks set at the previous conference. These tasks stem from each student's ability to internalize the different strategies modeled in the whole-class settings.

- Once the student has identified his or her goals, I ask a series of questions based on the goals. I may also ask the student to read part of the text to me to check his or her fluency, phrasing, and expression. If the student is unable to identify his or her reading goals, I remind the student what they were. At this stage, I usually end the conference because it's obvious that the student is not prepared. I reschedule the conference for another day and make sure the student works on established goals during independent reading.

- If the child is struggling with the set goals, I provide the appropriate scaffolds and make recommendations. I make sure I follow up with the child before the next conference so that I am not waiting an entire week to see whether the student has internalized the modeled strategies. This follow-up is not in the form of an additional conference, but more of an informal conversation. The conference with Jessica on pages 117–119 demonstrates this procedure.

- If the child appears to have accomplished the set goals, I congratulate him or her and set new goals. I record these goals in a notebook or conference record sheet. I also have the student record his or her new goals.

- If I find that I have several students struggling with specific strategies or goals, I call them together for small-group instruction. If I find that the majority of my students are struggling, I reintroduce the focus in a whole-class setting.

The following are two transcripts from conferences that demonstrate the previously described procedure. The first is with Jessica from Betty Mason's second-grade class. This conference shows what I do when a child is struggling with his or her set goals. The second is with Kirk from Peter's fifth-grade class. In this conference, Kirk has achieved his set goals, so I concentrate on other aspects of his reading.

Conference with Jessica in Grade 2

Focus: Selecting Texts That Are Comfortable Reads

Tony: Hi, Jessica. Would you like to tell me what you've been working on in your reading?

Jessica: Getting books that are right for me.

Tony: What do you mean, "books that are right"?

Jessica: Well, ones that I can read the words.

Tony: Do you think understanding what the words are saying is also important?

Jessica: Yeah.

Tony: Did you find any?

Jessica: I got three of 'em.

Tony: That's terrific. Would you like to read one of them to me?

Jessica begins reading a book about fish. Her reading of the text is slow and labored. She mispronounces many words. My running record reveals that this book is too hard for her. After she has read four pages, I stop her because she is struggling.

Tony: Jessica, I'm noticing that you are having problems with some of the words.

Jessica: Some of them are hard for me.

Tony: So do you find this is an easy book to read and understand?

Jessica: I can read some of it.

Tony: Do you understand it?

Jessica: Some bits.

Tony: That's great if you can understand some of it. Is there another book in your book bag that's a bit easier? Maybe a book where you can read nearly all of the words and understand what's happening?

Jessica: Well, I think that they could be a bit hard.

Tony: Then why don't you go back to the classroom library and find one that feels just right. Remember how we talked about using the chart to help you select comfortable texts?

I refer Jessica to the chart created in the whole-class mini-lesson. Refer to pages 93–94 in Chapter 6.

Tony: Do you think you can do that, Jessica? Or do you need more help? Maybe one of your friends can help you.

Jessica: I think I can do it.

Tony: That's terrific, Jessica. I'd like you to do that for me, and after I've finished my next conference, I'm going to come over to see how it's all going. Does that sound good?

Jessica: Yeah.

I write down Jessica's goals on her conference record sheet. I also write down the words: "I'm going to find something I can read and understand" on an index card and give it to Jessica. This is her record of her set goals. This is put into her book bag so that she has her own record of what she is going to be working on in her reading.

Tony: Okay, Jessica. I've written down in my notes that you are going to find a text that you can read and understand. I've written this on a card for you. It says, "I'm going to find something I can read and understand." So can you tell me what you're going to work on?

Jessica: Find something I know how to read.

Tony: And not only be able to read but also be able to . . .

Jessica: Understand.

Tony: Excellent. I'll be over soon to check how you're going.

At the end of my next conference, I go over to see how Jessica is doing. She has selected two books that appear easier. I congratulate her on her selections and ask her to find a few more. I tell her that when I meet with her next, I want her to bring one of her new selections to share at the conference. If Jessica had again struggled making appropriate selections, I would either have provided her with further support, or met with her in a small group with other children who were encountering the same problem.

Conference with Kirk in Grade 5

Focus: Reading Widely

Tony: Hi, Kirk. Can you tell me what you were working on in your reading?

Kirk: I had to find some different kinds of things to read.

Tony: What do you mean?

Kirk: Well I've been kind of reading lots of mysteries cuz I like 'em, but sometimes that's all I read. I found an article about water. It's about ways to save our planet. It's about global warming.

Tony: Sounds like a great article. Can you read a part that you found interesting?

Kirk: Sure.

He reads a section of the article that talks about the possible effects of global warming. He reads with good phrasing and intonation. I ask him to tell me what he has discovered from reading the article, and he gives me an excellent rendition of the article's content. It is evident that he understood the key points. I therefore move the discussions to making connections, which was the current focus of the share reading instruction. I want to see whether he is using this strategy as he reads.

Tony: That was great, Kirk. You know how we've been talking in whole-class discussions about making connections with what we read? Did you make any connections when you read this article?

Kirk: It made me think about using water better and about not using as much electricity.

Tony: Great. You've made a text-to-self connection. What about text-to-world connections?

Kirk: Well, I suppose the whole world has to be more careful; otherwise, we could ruin our planet. You know, the polar caps are melting and this can cause some cities to flood. It's not good for the polar bears either. They could die out.

Tony: What great world connections, Kirk. I want you to continue to read mysteries, because I know how much you love them. But I also want you to choose more articles on topics that you are interested in and continue to make connections with what you are reading. You may even want to read some other kinds of novels. Let's look at your reading log.

We examine Kirk's reading log, and I notice an absence of science fiction selections.

Tony: What about science fiction? Do you like these kinds of books?

Kirk: I've never really tried any. I think I should like them because I love watching *Star Wars* and *Star Trek*. You know I have the same name as one of the captains. He's called Captain Kirk from the *Starship Enterprise*.

Tony: That's amazing, Kirk. So tell me, what are you going to work on in your reading?

Kirk: I'm going to try a science fiction book. I'm going to get another article and make connections.

Tony: That's terrific, Kirk. Why don't you write down your goals, and I'll also write them down in my notes.

We can see in this transcript that Kirk's future goals are based not only on reading widely but also on the comprehension focus discussed in shared reading. As Peter or I continue to meet with Kirk, we will continue to broaden his reading diet by suggesting other text types. We will not discourage him from reading mysteries because these are the foundation for his love of reading.

Providing Specific Support Based on Individual Needs

Over the past twenty years, I have found that as I confer with different children in the selection process, a pattern of similar needs emerges. I have broken these into seven categories:

- The child who selects only texts that are too difficult
- The child who selects only texts that are too easy
- The struggling or reluctant reader
- The child who isn't reading widely
- The English as a second language learner
- The procrastinator
- The child who appears to need no support

The Child Who Selects Only Texts That Are Too Difficult

C.J., a third grader from Lisa Moynihan's classroom in New York, typified the child who selects texts that are too difficult. Even after constant individual and small-group scaffolds, C.J. had little success selecting reading material he could manage, partly because he was overwhelmed by the enormity of the task. I can relate to his reaction. When I walk into a bookstore, I can become lost in the sea of possibilities. To assist C.J., I narrowed down his available choices by gathering a number of texts from the classroom library. I carefully selected these texts based both on his interests and on his readability level. I informed C.J. that I had set up a special basket of books just for him. I named this collection the C.J. basket. He was very excited about having his own collection and was eager to begin selecting materials to read. Although he was still in control of the self-selection process, by narrowing down the field, I was making certain that he had materials he could read. As C.J. read through the collection, I added additional texts. I gave C.J. additional support through conferences that specifically focused on teaching him how to become a stronger reader by using a host of reading strategies. Eventually, C.J. was able to self-select texts from the classroom library, although he would continue to place these in his own basket. He loved having that special basket that was just his.

The Child Who Selects Only Texts That Are Too Easy

The student who selects materials that are too easy needs extra support too. Although reading materials within a child's comfort zone are suitable, an exclusive diet of easy-to-read material will do little to strengthen reading growth and stamina. A useful strategy is to select texts at a more complex reading level and invite them to choose one for independent reading.

Jenny, a fourth grader, constantly selected books at reading levels below her ability. I brought in several novels that I thought she might like and told her that I had selected these just for her and that no one else could borrow them. Her reaction to these books was instant. They were like rare and precious jewels. She selected *Tales of a Fourth-Grade Nothing* by Judy Blume and, after reading it, informed me that it was one of the best books she had read. I led her to other books by Judy Blume and, before long, she chose texts primarily at suitable readability levels. Jenny still selected some texts that were easy reads, but they were no longer the foundation of her independent reading.

The Struggling or Reluctant Reader

For me, conferencing with the at-risk child is the most difficult and yet the most rewarding experience. By third grade, these learners are usually aware that they are struggling readers. They often dislike reading and hide the fact that they are struggling. They pretend to read and are so effective that they can easily fade into the background. Robert was one of these learners I taught in sixth grade in inner-city Melbourne, Australia. At first I thought Robert was a competent reader. He appeared engaged during independent reading time. It was only when I called him up for an initial reading assessment that I realized how much he was struggling. My assessment indicated that he was reading at an early second-grade level; yet, he was selecting novels way above his independent reading level.

To provide assistance, we openly discussed his reading at his conference. Robert never directly admitted that he was struggling. He selected novels that his buddies read. He didn't want his peers to know that he was struggling, so each day he pretended to read. This is common with struggling readers in grades three through six. I knew the first plan of action was to get Robert to admit that he was having some problems and that he was willing to put in some effort to become a stronger reader. I achieved this by being direct. I told him that I knew he was having problems and had noticed he was selecting novels he couldn't read. I informed him that everyone struggled with something and that for me, it was drawing. I told him that I had never been good at art and had always received low grades. Although there are many things I have yet to master, I purposefully selected art as my failure because I knew that this was one of Robert's strengths. I told him how much I disliked having to draw or to paint but that I was willing to learn how to better my craft. I informed him that the way I felt about drawing was probably the way he felt about reading.

Robert was stunned by this admission. I don't think anyone in the past had shared that they too struggled at something. He became more at ease and told me that he was good at drawing and that it was not that hard if you tried. I told him that I felt the same way about reading. I asked him if he would be interested in teaching me how to draw, and if so I would repay the favor by helping him become a stronger reader. He was excited by this prospect so I drew up a contract to solidify our agreement. I arranged to have Robert meet with me twice a week, and during this time each of us would play the role of teacher to help the other become stronger at our identified crafts. I ensured that Robert had materials in his book bags that were at a suitable readability level and specifically chose nonfiction materials. Fictional selections at lower reading levels are inappropriate because they deal with plots and characters that are not developmentally suitable for the older student. They are too immature for a sixth-grade boy. Nonfiction, however, can provide stimulating and engaging content despite the readability level. I gave Robert home reading tasks, and he gave me drawing assignments to work on at home. To alleviate Robert's fears of being labeled by his peers, I allowed him to continue selecting more complex novels but stressed the importance of reading primarily nonfiction materials at suitable readability levels.

In addition to Robert's specific one-on-one reading instruction, I brought in a selection of engaging materials for him to choose from. I encouraged him to make his own selections from the classroom library and to use the chart "How to Select Suitable Texts," which we had constructed in whole-class mini-lessons, as a resource. It was a joy to see how quickly he progressed as a reader. I was also amazed that I mastered drawing. It challenged the adage that you can't teach an old dog new tricks. Within two months I was drawing objects I had never thought possible. It really does show that practice and engagement are the cornerstones of new learning.

The Child Who Isn't Reading Widely

As demonstrated in my conference with Kirk, the children who aren't reading widely usually requires a few recommendations by the teacher to extend their reading repertoire. However, one or two children may be locked into a specific genre or topic that they require additional scaffolds. This was certainly the case for Jonathon, a second-grade student who lived and breathed cars and trucks. If the text was not about an automobile, he had no interest in it. At first, I recommended or brought in books about animals, space, and sports for him to select, but unless they had wheels he had little interest.

I changed my tactic, and rather than recommending texts to him, I asked him to recommend texts to me. I told him that just as he loved cars and trucks, I liked texts about animals, specifically bears, tigers, monkeys, and kangaroos. I told him that I knew a lot about these creatures and that if he found any books that could give me more information I would be grateful. I asked him to make sure he read through these books first to see whether there was great information that he thought might interest me. I let him know that if he didn't have time to do this, I could ask someone else in the class to assist me. This was an invitation Jonathon couldn't refuse.

At our following conference, he brought ten books for me to read. He had diligently read them all and told me that there were five he thought I would really like because they had interesting information. I thanked him and asked him whether he enjoyed reading the books. He told me that he did, so I recommended that he might like to select some materials to read on these creatures, and we could discuss all the facts he had discovered at our next conference. This would be our special animals club. I encourage him to find books about other creatures that I would be interested in reading about. Texts on animals soon became a stable part of his reading routine. At later conferences, I extended Jonathan's reading diet by asking him to locate books on other topics. These included stories and poems. Jonathan continued to select books about trucks and cars, but he also included a range of different texts.

Allowing time for children to share their reading logs and to make recommendations to one another is also a valuable means for extending their reading selections. At least once every two weeks, I paired children up and asked them to recommend a text they thought their partner might be interested in reading. To help extend their reading diet, I paired children who read different types of texts so that they were exposed to different genres and topics.

The English as a Second Language Learner

English as a second language learners can often require additional support in the conference, especially with selecting suitable texts. Many of these students, especially older readers who learn how to pronounce words quickly, select texts they can decode, but they struggle with comprehension. When I began to learn Italian, it didn't take long before I became a fluent decoder of the language. I could easily pick up any printed materials and read it with ease, even though I had no clue what the words actually meant.

To assist English as a second language learners, I ask them to always be prepared to talk about the materials they bring to conference. I impress on them the importance of not only reading words but also understanding the message. Nonfiction materials are great selections for English as a second language learners for two reasons. First, as with the struggling readers, nonfiction materials provide developmentally appropriate content despite the level of text complexity.

Second, and contrary to popular belief, nonfiction can often be easier to comprehend than fiction. In many nonfiction texts, and especially in descriptions, much of the information is presented as a series of facts. The reader is therefore able to gather small chunks of meaning. Each fact is not necessarily dependent on the surrounding facts to make meaning. Take, for instance, the following information about dragonflies from the book *Dragonflies Are Amazing* by Marie Powell.

> *Dragonflies have five eyes! They have four wings! They are among the largest insects on Earth. Dragonflies are truly amazing. Around the world, people have always been fascinated with dragonflies. They got their name because some people thought they looked like fierce dragons. Even though they look fierce, dragonflies do not sting or bite humans or other animals, and they do not harm plants.*

In reading this piece, it is not necessary for the reader to understand the meaning of every word or sentence to gather information. Naturally, the more words the student understands, the more information they can acquire. Even though many of these facts relate to one another, more than eight separate pieces of information are presented. Therefore, even if readers understand only a few of the facts presented, they still have made some form of meaning. In fiction, however, the reader needs to understand most of the small chunks of information presented to understand characters, sequence of events, and plot. If meaning is lost after the first few sentences, then the reader will find it difficult to understand the remainder of the story.

Apart from encouraging English as a second language learners to include nonfiction in their selections, I find books on tape are great choices for these students because it assists them in the acquisition of oral language, which is the foundation of reading comprehension. I often keep with me a selection of books on tape rather than putting them all in the classroom library. In this way, I always have some on hand to recommend to English as a second language learners who are struggling with comprehension. It is important to encourage English as a second language learners to borrow familiar texts that have been previously introduced in read-aloud and shared reading encounters.

The Procrastinator

The procrastinator finds it difficult to make a selection. Like the kid in the candy store the procrastinator becomes overwhelmed by possibilities. Some procrastinators simply want to read everything they see and will pick up ten to twenty books, and then spend twenty minutes trying to decide which ones to select. To assist these learners, I ask them to put the texts they are deciding on borrowing into one pile and then to select every fifth book in the pile. These then become their weekly selections. They can either write down the titles of the others and select these in the future or put them back into the classroom library and repeat the process of selecting every fifth text the next time they borrow. It really doesn't need to be every fifth book. It could be every second or third. I have used this strategy for a number of years and found it to be highly successful, for it encourages the procrastinator to get down to reading and not spend all their time selecting.

Establishing a "Record of Books and Magazines I Want to Read," as discussed and shown in Figure 1.4 in Chapter 1, is also a great strategy to help procrastinators make timely decisions. By simply recording all the texts they intend to read, they can actually start reading and not just collate possibilities. This record assisted Kelly, who was the queen of all procrastinators, in my sixth-grade classroom. Kelly would take up to one hour to make her selections. Her mother informed me that when they visited a bookstore Kelly had to be physically dragged out after two hours, with no book because she couldn't make up her mind. To support

Kelly, I knew I had to put a solid structure in place. In the conference, I told her that when it was her day for borrowing she had to write down her intended selections on note cards and number these 1 through 10. I limited the number to ten because Kelly ended up with twenty to thirty possible selections each time. I had Kelly randomly pull out four note cards from a pile numbered 1 through 10. The four numbers became her weekly selections. This proved to be highly successful. Kelly loved this game of chance and before long would simply shuffle the cards and do this alone when it was her turn to borrow.

The Child Who Appears to Need No Support

The question I often wrestled with is what to do with students who are able to select appropriate texts, read widely, and connect with everything they read. What is the function of the conferences, apart from just spot-checking that everything is in order with their independent reading? I was faced with this predicament when I worked with Peter in his fifth-grade classroom. Five fluent readers in his class appeared to need no support. They had internalized all the strategies in selecting appropriate texts and reading widely as provided in whole-class mini-lessons. The conference with these students became a frustrating and useless process of trying to find something for them to work on in their reading.

Peter and I informed these students that they would no longer need to attend weekly conferences unless we specifically requested a meeting to spot-check how their independent reading was progressing. We reasoned that the time spent conferencing with these students was best allocated to more at-risk students. A week later the group asked to meet with us because they had something they wanted to discuss. Intrigued by their request, we brought the students together to find out what was troubling them. They informed us that they didn't think it was fair that they were missing out on their weekly conference. We told them how we thought that they were such strong readers that we found it difficult to find a focus for their conferences.

What they told us next made me reevaluate the function of these conferences. They loved coming to these conferences to share their reading in a one-to-one interaction. Peter and I realized that apart from monitoring his students' internalization of strategies introduced in whole-class mini-lessons, the conference was a valued one-on-one opportunity for his students to discuss their reading. It was their special time with the teacher. We apologized to them for our hasty decision and reinstated this special time. We asked them what they thought the focus of these conferences should be. Their response was simple: to talk about what they had been reading. They wanted to chat about books. They were proud learners who wanted to share their latest endeavors as readers. They also asked if they could recommend to us great texts they had read for consideration in whole-class read-alouds. This was such a powerful moment for me as an educator. It reaffirmed the belief that students need to be part of the decision-making process. We need to encourage them to be active learners who take responsibility for their learning.

Their revelation inspired Peter and me to explore ways to take these learners to new heights. Because they were reading well above grade level did not mean they had no more to learn. As Ellin Keene suggests, we needed to "raise the bar." Peter and I introduced these learners to not only more complex materials but also texts that dealt with points of view and author bias such as articles, editorials, and newspaper clippings. We wanted to develop their strategies in critical perspective.

Procedures in Ongoing Monitoring and Record-Keeping

Meeting with as many as twenty-eight children over the course of a week requires solid ongoing monitoring procedures. It can be easy to lose track of individual goals and needs if concrete and manageable record-keeping procedures are not in place. Some suggestions follow.

Teacher Conference Notes

Keeping a record of conferences allows the teacher to keep track of each child's goals. They are a wonderful reference point when the child comes to conference because they enable the teacher to begin the conference by directly focusing on previous goals set. Like a journal, they are an ongoing record of what has been discussed over the course of the year in each child's independent reading. There are many ways to maintain conference notes. One way is to simply keep conference sheets for each child as shown in Figure 7.7. The notes on each child can be housed in separate folders, or these notes can be kept in spiral notebooks. Refer to Appendix Q for a copy you may wish you use.

Independent Reading Monitoring Rubric

Using a monitoring rubric as shown in Figure 7.8 is an effective tool for keeping track of how children individually internalize the strategies introduced in whole-class settings. Refer to Appendix R for an example

Figure 7.7
A Record of Conference Notes

Name Juan De Castro   Grade 2

Date	Conference Notes
9/6/07	Juan will find a suitable book to read
9/14/07	Juan will try to find 3 suitable texts
9/20/07	Juan will borrow a nonfiction piece
9/27/07	Juan is going to make sure he can read and understand the nonfiction text he borrows
10/3/07	Juan is going to have 2 fiction and 2 nonfiction texts that he can read and understand.
10/10/07	Juan is going to pick a magazine to read.
10/17/07	Juan is going to use his strategies when he comes to words he doesn't know the meaning of.
10/24/07	Juan is going to try to select books about animals and space
11/7/07	Juan is going to try to read a book from the Magic Tree House series
11/14/07	Juan has decided to read more of the magic tree house series. He will also select some nonfiction to read.
11/21/07	Juan is going to continue with the magic tree house. For his nonfiction selection he is going to read an article

of an independent reading rubric. By including a key on the rubric, I was able to record gradients of each child's understandings. As Figure 7.8 shows, I was able to see how Juan had progressed over a five-month period in key strategies. I had a clear direction on what he had consolidated and his future needs. These monitoring rubrics can be housed in the folders that contain the conference notes.

Good Choice!

Observation Rubric for Independent Reading	Key:				
Months of: OCTOBER - FEBRUARY	**1** Not in evidence				
	2 Showing signs of				
Child's Name: Juan De Castro	**3** Strengthening				
Grade: 2	**4** Nearly always				

Date	OCT	NOV	DEC	JAN	FEB
Selects fiction texts for independent reading	2	3	4	4	4
Selects nonfiction texts for independent reading	1	2	2	3	4
Able to select fiction material at appropriate readability levels	1	2	2	3	3
Able to select nonfiction material at appropriate readability levels	1	1	2	2	2
Reads widely with fiction, e.g., fantasy, fables, adventures, mysteries, science fiction, realistic fiction	1	1	2	2	3
Reads widely with nonfiction, e.g., biographies, magazines, maps, articles, descriptions, procedures, persuasions	1	2	2	2	3
Can talk about information read	2	3	3	3	3
Has built up stamina for independently reading fiction	2	3	3	3	3
Has built up stamina for independently reading nonfiction	1	2	2	2	2
Reads with fluency	1	2	2	2	3
Reads with expression	1	2	2	3	3
Able to gain information from pictures and photographs	1	2	2	3	3
Able to interpret information from illustrative sources such as tables, graphs, and maps	1	2	2	2	2
Uses strategies to work out the meaning of unknown words	1	2	2	2	3

Additional Comments

Work on selecting appropriate nonfiction materials

Needs to build up stamina

Revisit strategies for unknown vocabulary

Figure 7.8 Independent Reading Monitoring Rubric

Students Keeping Their Own Records

In addition to teachers keeping records of their students' accomplishments and goals, students should keep their own records. Learners need to be active participants in the learning process, which includes keeping track of their own reading. We need to lead our students to become responsible and independent learners. When I worked with Lisa Moynihan in her third-grade class, we gave each student a reading binder, as shown in Figure 7.9. These reading binders were divided into four sections as described here.

Section One
This houses the students'
- Reading logs (see Chapter 1, page 11)
- Books and materials they want to read (see Chapter 1, page 12)

Section Two: My Goals
The students record their goals after the individual conference. This gives them a quick reference point in case they forget what they should be working on in their independent reading. See Figure 7.10, and refer to Appendix S for a record of goals you may wish to give to your students. In addition to recording goals set in independent reading, Lisa and I also had the students record their goals after guided reading encounters.

Section Three: Strategy Charts
This section in the reading binder contains examples of the charts constructed during whole-class mini-lessons, such as those discussed earlier

Figure 7.9
Reading Binders

Good Choice!

Figure 7.10
Maggie's Reading
Goals

| Name Maggie Gao | Grade 4 |

Date	Goals To Work On In My Reading
9/8	I will choose some fiction and some non-fiction
9/15	I will get non-fiction that I can understand
9/22	I will try to use my strategys for words I don't know I will get nonfiction I like.
9/30	I will try to find a novel by a new author.
10/6	I will get books about horses to help me with my research.
10/12	I will read some more Judy Blume because I like her
10/17	I'm going to try some different kinds of non-fiction like how to's
10/25	I'm going to read more how to's because I love them

in the chapter (see Figures 7.5 and 7.6). It was essential that each student have a copy of any chart we had constructed together as a class in their reading binders. Often we construct wonderful charts and display them in the classroom; however, students find it overwhelming trying to locate the information. It becomes lost in a sea of classroom print. At one point, I had more than forty charts displayed in my classroom. It was overwhelming. There was no room to display all these charts, and they were not always on hand for each child to refer to, whether at school or at home. With the students keeping their own copies, I am able to make room for other displays and to have a less cluttered classroom.

Section Four: Responses
This section of the reading binder contains the students' responses to literature. This will be discussed in detail in Chapters 9 and 10.

Lisa and I found that the reading binders were very popular and were a wonderful way to assist the students in keeping their notes, charts, and logs organized and in one central location. Initially we had simply used manila folders but decided to give them something more special. We made the right decision because the students treasured them. They felt grown up and professional by having their own special binder. Many commented that they felt like middle or high school students. They decorated the covers, and some students even added extra sections. I have since shared this concept of reading binders with many teachers and have received encouraging feedback. Gina Sheehan, a multiage grades three and four teacher from Twin Valley Elementary School in Pennsylvania, told me that it has been one of the best tools she has adopted. Binders helped her students become more responsible and organized learners.

8

The Question of Readability Levels

I n the second edition of *Beyond Leveled Books*, Karen Szymusiak, Franki Sibberson, and Lisa Koch address the growing popularity of leveled books:

> Along the way, this well-intentioned knowledge base gradually became a way to measure a reader's progress. Levels became more important than the features of books that could support or challenge a reader. Instead of a useful part of the information Fountas and Pinnell had so clearly identified for teachers, the levels became invisible badges that students wore to enter a not-so-invisible race. The goal had changed from recognizing books that support readers to moving up the levels to claim some sense of accomplishment. Children, parents, and some teachers began to focus on moving to higher levels instead of paying attention to what readers were doing and how particular books supported them.

133

We never intended for children to use levels to choose books. But across the country, teachers began sorting their entire classroom libraries into leveled baskets. (2008, 13–14)

For many years, leveling much of my classroom library governed my thinking. Even with appropriate scaffolds, as discussed in the previous two chapters, many of my children, especially my beginning readers, still found it difficult to self-select appropriate material for independent reading. They needed more time and opportunities until they were comfortable with the self-selection process. This could take time, and meanwhile I was faced with children reading inappropriate materials. Therefore, I provided additional support by leveling and coding the materials in my classroom library.

Indeed, this is what many school districts have done. Much of their classroom libraries are organized by level and have colored labels on the baskets to signify the degrees of difficulty. Many teachers call these baskets A, B, C, and so on, based on the Fountas and Pinnell leveling system. I used their system of leveling books to organize much of my classroom library. Books deemed suitable for my early emergent readers were placed in baskets, and these baskets were labeled yellow. All the books in these baskets had a yellow sticker on the back. Eventually, I had ten to twelve baskets of books at different readability levels with color codes to signify their complexity. I still had some baskets organized by topic, but most of my classroom library was organized by level. This proved effective because I could confer with my children and assist them select books at their desired independent reading level by directly referring them to books with a specific color code.

However, my beliefs and understandings of helping children select appropriate material based primarily on level were challenged one day in a conference with Sebastian, a first-grade student. Sebastian was an early emergent reader who, through conferences, had understood that books in the yellow baskets were just right for him. He knew that he could also select a few texts that had a higher-level color code because he could get information from the pictures, or because they were familiar texts that he had heard before. However, he understood that the majority of his selections needed to be from the yellow baskets because these materials were most suitable for independent reading. On this particular day at the conference, I asked Sebastian whether he had made his selections for independent reading. He replied, "Not yet. I know that books from the yellow basket are just right for me, but I hope there's a book on spiders in there. I love spiders."

His statement gnawed at my existing beliefs. I had put his readability level over his interests. I had forgotten that in independent reading a child's interests should rule. He was reading to please to me, not for self-enjoyment. Children still need to select books they can read, but their interests need to be the initial part of the selection process.

By having all the books with a yellow sticker housed together I was giving children such as Sebastian limited access to many of the baskets in the classroom library. They had become the forbidden fruits and therefore more desirable. I reorganized my classroom library using interest topics and themes as described in Chapter 3 and then color-coded around 30 percent of the books within each of these baskets to give my learners a secondary layer of support when making selections. In this way, my students had access to all the baskets in the library but knew that an array of materials would be available at different levels. The colored stickers could give them support in making wise selections. As I reorganized my baskets by topic and looked at the readability levels within each basket, I came to a startling realization. Most of the materials that had yellow stickers on them and represented my early level books were simple narratives, whereas the materials that had a blue code and represented my more complex texts were primarily nonfiction materials. Therefore, the majority of my nonfiction materials were at readability levels above where most of my children could read. For children like Sebastian, this meant rarely reading nonfiction at a level of comfort. Sebastian's prime selections were fiction despite his high interest in informational texts. This insight ensured that when I did purchase nonfiction materials, I looked at the readability levels of these so that all my children would have access to suitable texts.

The coding system I use and the percentage of leveled books within each basket depend on a number of factors, namely, the grade area and children's past experiences in selecting appropriate texts. Between 20 and 30 percent of books in first-grade baskets might be leveled, whereas in fifth grade, this percentage may be substantially lower or not necessary. The particular colors used to code materials are not relevant. What is important is that some type of system is in place that acts as a secondary support system if students find they are having difficulties selecting suitable texts. I call this a secondary support because the goal is to have them use strategies as outlined in Chapter 6 as their prime support. They need to know that when selecting reading material from, let's say, the "Oceans" basket, they should look through the text to see whether they can read and understand it. If they are still having difficulty with the selection process, then they need to know to check the basket for books with a colored dot to signify the material's degree of difficulty.

Leveling raises many issues. Some helpful ideas follow. They are organized under grade-area headings because many issues are largely dependent on children's past experience in selecting texts and their level of competencies as readers. Within each grade area, different issues arise.

Kindergarten and Early Grade 1

In most kindergartens and in those first-grade classrooms in which children have not received kindergarten instruction, more than 90 percent of the children could be pre-emergent readers. Many children may have early knowledge of concepts about print with some letter/sound knowledge; however, their ability to sit down with a book and actually read and comprehend the print will be limited. Many children will be able to look through the pictures and invent content. Indeed, children who have been read to at home should be successful with inventing content. Before he entered school, my son would sit for extended periods of time inventing complex plots based entirely on the pictures. When tackling nonfiction pieces, he used the illustrations to make up his own facts, oblivious to the information presented in the formal print. When it came to books that I had read to him countless times before, he would no longer simply use the pictures to invent. He would recite word for word each page of the book. When I reread such books to him, he would stop me if I mispronounced a word. "It doesn't say that, Papa" would spring from his mouth, and I wasn't allowed to continue until I had corrected my miscue.

Pre-emergent readers who have been read to realize that a book tells a story, whether it is fictional or factual. That they cannot read the words is no barrier because they use the pictures or memorize the print to make meaning. Therefore, many of the books in the topic baskets will need to be texts that have been read to students during read-aloud experiences and books they have encountered during shared reading experiences. In Clara's kindergarten classroom, we always ensured that when reading a Big Book, let's say on sharks, some small copies of the book were available in the "Oceans" basket for students to borrow and read. At the conclusion of our shared readings, we always informed the children that copies of the book we had read were available and where they were housed. We encouraged them to borrow these during independent and buddy reading time. Simple texts that have high picture support are also suitable for these learners as they will be able to make up stories and talk about facts by using the illustrations. Color-coding books is ineffective for the pre-emergent reader because the codes offer no support in the selection process. It is better to have a range of simple books with high picture support and copies of texts that have been introduced in read-aloud and shared reading encounters placed in topic baskets.

But what about the pre-emergent readers who have not had many experiences with being read to at home, or children who are English as a second language learners? They too will benefit from having a copy of a book introduced during a read-aloud and shared reading encounter. Reading texts to and with children in whole-class settings will give them enough support to begin talking about the book's content. The teacher needs to provide these children with encounters with books that were missing before they entered the classroom and to make copies of these texts available for them to use during independent reading. These children will also find simple texts with suitable high picture support if they know how to tell the story using illustrations. Teacher demonstrations will be a key factor in assisting these children.

Providing read-aloud, shared reading, and simple texts with high picture support alleviates the problem experienced in many kindergarten and early grade-one classrooms where children have difficulty staying on task during independent reading time. I constantly hear from kindergarten teachers that independent reading time lasts for only three minutes and that the children quickly become disengaged with books. When I look in the classroom library it is not surprising why this is occurring. The texts are at high readability levels with no evidence that they were first introduced during read-aloud and shared reading encounters. As teachers, we need to ensure that when we do purchase read-aloud texts we buy several copies: one that can be kept from the hands of babes so that we always have a good copy to read-aloud for years to come and at least two for students to select from during independent reading time. It's almost cruel when teachers read wonderful books to children and then stash them away. It's akin to showing them a fabulous toy but not letting them play with it. The same can be said for our shared readings. I would much prefer to have five Big Books, together with six small copies of the text, than twenty Big Books. Children need to read independently and buddy-read familiar texts if they are to become competent and confident readers.

Besides the pre-emergent readers entering the kindergarten classroom, a small percentage of children can independently read print. Their reading levels will become evident from the teachers' preassessments. In addition to books that have been introduced during read-aloud and shared reading encounters, texts at their appropriate level are also needed. It is necessary to code some of the material in the topic baskets to ensure that these learners not only have texts they have seen before in whole-class settings but also unseen texts they can independently read with success.

This was certainly the case in Linda Hadley's kindergarten classroom. Her preassessments showed that eighteen of the twenty-five

Figure 8.1
Children's Levels After
Preassessments

Child's Name	F/P Level	DRA Level
Sammy	A	A–1
Laura	A	A–1
Sally	B	2
Sara	B	2
Melissa	C	3–4
Franco	D	4–6
Catherine	F	10

children were pre-emergent readers who would require read-aloud and shared reading books together with simple texts with high picture support for independent reading. However, seven children were emergent readers. Their reading levels after preassessments are listed in Figure 8.1. I have used Fountas and Pinnell (F/P), and Directed Reading Assessment (DRA) levels because these are the ones most commonly used by school districts and were the ones used by Linda in her preassessments.

As seen in Figure 8.1, to ensure that her emergent readers had suitable materials, it was necessary to have a variety of texts, ranging between Fountas and Pinnell levels A through G in the topic baskets. These were coded for easy identification and access. Linda and I coded some of the books in each topic basket with either a yellow, blue, or green dot on the back, as seen in Figure 8.2. Books that were deemed above level H were not initially coded.

During conferences (see Chapter 7 for more details), Linda was able to suggest to Sammy, Laura, Sally, and Sara that in addition to selecting favorite read-alouds and shared reading from the interest baskets, books with a yellow dot on the back would also be suitable selections. In the case of Melissa and Franco, books with both yellow and blue dots would be appropriate. Catherine would benefit from having some books with green dots, although books with yellow and blue dots would also be wise selections because they were well within her comfort

Figure 8.2
Linda's Color Codes
Matched with Fountas
and Pinnell Levels

Color Code	Approximate F/P Level
Yellow	A and B
Blue	C and D
Green	E, F, and G

zone. During independent reading time, children who can read should be connecting with texts well within their comfort zone, not just materials at their level.

Linda was also aware that eventually she would have most of her pre-emergent readers becoming emergent and would therefore need many books at levels A and B to cater to these learners. Franco and Catherine would also need more challenging texts as they grew as readers, so eventually Linda introduced a new color code that had texts between levels H and J.

In Mandy Carlson's kindergarten classroom, color coding of some of the texts in the classroom library was handled differently. Mandy found from her preassessments that only two children were emergent readers. The remainder of the class were pre-emergent. Mandy had been teaching for some time and had accumulated many books for her classroom library. She was aware that most children in kindergarten read between the range of Fountas and Pinnell's A through D. Therefore, the majority of the literature she had amassed were at these early levels. Rather than code some of these materials, she simply coded all the texts that were above level D with a blue sticker. She informed her children that a book with a blue sticker on the back meant they could obtain information from the pictures because the words might be too difficult. As her children became emergent readers, she led them to selections that were at a suitable level.

Mandy knew her children, but more importantly she knew the books in her collection. This is critical because if the classroom library has too many texts that are at high readability levels children can become overwhelmed with the selection process. When my son was three years old, I took him to FAO Schwarz in New York, which at that time was one of the largest toy stores in the world. His excitement was reflected in his saucer-like eyes. He had entered utopia. I told him I would let him choose something to buy and then asked him to make a selection. My wife shook her head in disbelief at this invitation. I soon realized why. Within minutes he began to cry. He was overwhelmed by the choices. My wife took him by the hand and said to me, "Now watch the master." She led him to the section with Thomas the Tank Engine paraphernalia, for she knew he loved Thomas and all the other engines. She showed him several different engines, which included Thomas, James, and Henry. She then asked him which one he would like. He selected Thomas, and the smile reappeared on his face. My wife *was* the master. She had made the selection process easy. The classroom library is no different. We need to include primarily texts that are around children's comfort levels. Mandy had achieved this by having most of her classroom library at those early levels but then coding challenging materials.

Grades 1 and 2

First- and second-grade classrooms can be the most challenging when leveling some of the texts in the topic baskets. The difficulty arises from the enormous range of readability levels among students. Consider Laura Ramos's first-grade class. As seen in Figure 8.3, her midyear assessments indicated the following range of readability levels.

The dilemma confronting Laura is clear. To cater to the wide range of reading abilities among her students, she needed a variety of color codes to provide guidance for all her learners. To accomplish this, we used color codes as shown in Figure 8.4.

As seen in Figure 8.4, Laura and I were attempting to provide independent reading materials for all of her children within an approximate range of their comfort zone. I say "approximate" because children cannot be labeled as reading at a level; rather, they are operating within a range of texts that signifies their reading stage of development. I have used the reading stages (shown in Figure 8.4) with the corresponding levels for over ten years. These stages are based on the work of and discussions with many educators. They are not set in stone. Different school districts, teacher educators, and publishing companies often use

Figure 8.3
Readability Levels from Midyear Assessments

Name	F/P Level	DRA Level	Name	F/P Level	DRA Level
Crystal	A	A–1	Natalie	F	10
Steven	A	A–1	Smiley	F	10
Stephanie	B	2	Diana	F	10
John G.	B	2	Sebastian	G	12
Miguel	D	4–6	Julio	G	12
Jeffrey	D	4–6	Nabila	G	12
Vladimir	D	4–6	Katiosca	G	12
John M.	D	4–6	Carmen	G	12
Nicole	D	4–6	Victor	H	14
Daniel	E	6–8	Daven	H	14
Elaine	E	6–8	Anthony	I	16
Anasia	E	6–8	Alexandra	I	16
Faria	F	10	Michelle	J	18
Katherine	F	10	Brian	L	24
Oswald	F	10	Jonathan	M	24–28

Figure 8.4
Laura's Color Codes
Matched with Specific
Reading Stages and
Fountas and Pinnell
Levels

Color Code	Reading Stage	Approximate F and P Level
Yellow	Early emergent	A, B, and C
Blue	Emergent	C, D, E, and F
Green	Early reader	F, G, H, and I
Red	Transitional	I, J, K, and L
Orange	Early fluency	L. M, N, O
No color code	Fluent	O Plus

different terminology to describe the developmental stages of reading and their corresponding levels.

Laura also realized that her children shouldn't be locked into reading only materials at their developmental reading stage. Even though books with a green dot on the back should make up the bulk of materials for early readers in their independent reading, materials with yellow and blue dots were also suitable selections. Independent reading is not just about having texts that are at a child's level but also having texts well within a child's comfort zone.

Many children may also find suitable texts at higher levels than indicated by assessments. This is especially true for nonfiction when children have strong background knowledge about a specific topic, which was the case for Oswald in Laura's classroom. His assessments indicated that he was operating at around a Fountas and Pinnell E and F; yet, he was easily able to navigate a text on frogs that was leveled H because he had solid background knowledge about frogs, which were his favorite animal.

As in Linda's kindergarten, Laura did not code all the materials in her classroom library, maybe between 25 and 30 percent. Her children were provided with ongoing demonstrations on how to select suitable texts, and she encouraged them to use these strategies first. It was only when her learners encountered difficulties that the color codes became a secondary support.

Grades 2 and 3

By late second grade and early into third grade, many children will be moving from being transitional readers into early fluency. How necessary, then, is it to color-code some of the materials in the classroom library? The answer depends on the children's abilities to self-select

Figure 8.5

Katie's Color Codes Matched with Specific Reading Stages

Color Code	Reading Stage	Approximate F and P Level
Green	Early reader	F, G, H, and I
Red	Transitional	I, J, K, and L
Orange	Early fluency	L, M, N, and O

materials that they can read and comprehend. However, transitional readers may still need additional support in the selection process.

In Katie Zerbo's third-grade classroom, we found after her initial assessments that around a third of her children were transitional readers. Most of them struggled with selecting appropriate materials for independent reading because they had encountered limited demonstrations in previous years on how to select materials. Katie's assessments also indicated that four of her children were struggling readers who were operating in the early reader developmental stage. Not surprisingly, these children also struggled in the selection process. The remainder of Katie's children were either early fluent or fluent readers. Most of them, especially the fluent readers, appeared able to locate suitable text from the classroom library, which supported the notion that once readers become fluent they will look for texts they can read. The challenge with many of the fluent readers was their nonfiction selections. Typically, they would select texts that were too hard for them to comprehend and relied primarily on the illustrations in the materials to gain information.

We initiated discussion with the class on how to select appropriate texts as outlined in Chapter 6 and then used color codes as seen in Figure 8.5 as a secondary layer of support. We coded approximately 15 percent of the books in each topic basket but put no codes on books that were housed together as part of a series, such as The Magic School Bus. Through continued demonstrations, most of the children would eventually be able to select appropriate materials; therefore, only a small percentage of books needed coding to initially assist the children with the selection process. For our fluent readers, we knew that helping them select appropriate nonfiction texts was best achieved through conversations in conferences and that color codes were not needed.

Grades 3–6

With proper scaffolds in years kindergarten through three, by the end of grade three, most children should be able to select appropriate texts.

Peter Miller, a fifth-grade teacher, said it perfectly: "Tony, my children know when they pick up a book if it's too hard for them. We've had many conversations about this. For the most part they are all fluent readers. Color coding doesn't help them or me. What they need are ongoing demonstrations in selecting a wide range of materials so they don't get locked into only selecting texts in too narrow a field."

Peter's comments are valid, especially when we consider that when children enter middle school or their local public library there is no color coding system in place. By the time children become fluent readers, they should be competent in using strategies to help them make wise decisions about what they are able to read and comprehend. For those few children still struggling with the selection process, individual support through conferences as discussed in the previous chapter is a better option.

Although Peter's students were competent in the selection process they do not represent all learners in grades four through six. Many children appear to struggle with locating appropriate texts due to lack of demonstrations and experiences in previous years. Even though many of these learners are fluent, simply providing demonstrations in the selection process will not magically rectify the situation. They need time to internalize and practice the demonstrations. When I taught sixth grade, most of my children were fluent readers; yet, they selected books that were too difficult for them to comprehend. They could decode the words but missed out on much of the meaning because of challenging vocabulary and concepts. I talked with them about what constituted a suitable text for independent reading, but they continued to struggle with making their individual selections. This was because of the lack of experiences in previous years and because of the huge range of materials at different levels in my classroom library. Although my students were taking the time to look through materials when making selections, they were overwhelmed by looking through countless books to locate a suitable choice, much like my son was in FAO Schwarz, as discussed earlier in this chapter.

To assist them, we decided as a class to look through the classroom library and place blue dots on the back of challenging material. My students were responsible for this project because they were willing and able, and needed to be accountable for the organizational process. Sorting texts proved enlightening. I had accumulated many books, particularly novels that were challenging for the majority of my sixth graders. I weeded out some of these materials from the collection for later in the year when they would be less challenging for my students. I retained most of the challenging nonfiction titles because my students would extract information from the visual elements such as illustrations, charts, maps, and tables. This strategy appeared effective, and I noticed that my students immediately began selecting more suitable texts. Rather than using colored dots, some teachers I have worked with in grades four through six place more challenging texts together in baskets or containers and label them "More Challenging Novels" and "More Challenging Nonfiction."

Commonly Asked Questions

As I have worked with teachers individually in their classrooms, in workshops, and in conferences, I am constantly asked questions about the leveling of texts for independent reading. These are discussed here.

If I decide to color-code some of the material in my classroom library, how do I proceed?
For many teachers, especially in the early years, having to code some of their materials in the classroom library is not a pleasant thought. Depending on the quantity of materials in the classroom library, the amount of time needed to complete such a task could be extensive. To try and complete this within the first weeks of the school year is unrealistic. The process is ongoing, but once completed only new materials purchased may need coding.

Before coding, it is essential to look at your preassessment to determine the range of levels that exist within your classroom and then decide on the leveling system you are going to use. Many are available, but I have found that Reading Recovery, Fountas and Pinnell, and DRA are the ones most commonly used by school districts. Most publishers also use these leveling systems, which makes it easier for coding existing books and for purchasing new material.

The next step is to determine which colors will represent which range of materials and then code them. I have seen teachers have breakdowns trying to achieve this. They fear they might have books incorrectly coded. My answer to this dilemma is, "Who cares?" We need to remember that the color codes are only a secondary guide for the purpose of giving some children extra support when selecting materials for independent reading. If you or the children discover a book that was coded blue is better as a yellow, then change it.

How do I know what level a book is when I am color coding?
The good news is that most publishers now indicate an approximate level of their materials using Reading Recovery, Fountas and Pinnell, and DRA levels. I have also found the publication *Guided Reading:*

Good First Teaching for All Children (1996) by Fountas and Pinnell to be a valuable resource that outlines key characteristics of books at different levels. Their publications *Matching Books to Readers* (1999), *Guiding Readers and Writers Grades 3–6* (2001), and *Leveled Books for Readers Grades 3–6* (2002) also give the approximate reading levels of thousands of books. For teachers in Canada, Scholastic's *Literacy Place for the Early Years* (Brailsford and Stead 2007), and *Moving Up with Literacy Place* (Brailsford and Stead 2008) also give key characteristics of books at different levels. When leveling texts, do not get locked into trying to decide whether a book is at a specific level but rather whether it is within a range of levels.

If I decide to color-code some of my books, what percentage should be coded?
There is no magical percentage because it depends on the range of readability levels within the classroom and children's aptitude to select appropriate materials. From my own experiences, and discussions with other educators, 5 to 30 percent is ample. With learners in grades four through six, this percentage may be as low as 5 percent, or color coding may not even be needed.

Does it matter what color codes I use?
The color codes used are not important. Some schools have found it advantageous to have a consistency between grade areas. For example, materials suitable for emergent readers at Fountas and Pinnell levels C through F are coded with a specific color. The advantage of this is that children don't get confused with different color codes each year. The disadvantage is that in kindergarten and in early grade one, there are many early emergent readers, and using one color code to represent more than two levels may be too broad and not provide enough support for these learners. In Linda's kindergarten classroom (discussed earlier in the chapter), there is a significant difference in children's abilities to access books at a Fountas and Pinnell A and B compared with a C and D; therefore, Linda coded her A and B material yellow and her C and D books blue. In comparison, Laura, a first-grade teacher, used a broader range of levels for her early emergent readers, as she only had three children in need of these texts and knew that through conferencing could assist them with wise selections.

I have books that the publishers are telling me are at a specific level; yet, they seem too difficult for the children borrowing them, even though these children are reading around that level. What do I do?
Books already leveled by publishers can act as a good guide in deciding which color codes should be placed on particular books; however, we

must be careful not to rely solely on publishers to tell us which texts are more difficult than others. We need to know that the supports and challenges of particular texts, together with the background experiences of our children, are important factors when making decisions on color coding. If you think a book is incorrectly leveled, then change it. Another consideration when relying on publisher's levels is that each publisher does not use the same set of people when leveling their books. Consequently, what one publisher calls suitable for emergent readers, another calls appropriate for early readers.

How do I level nonbook resources?

Although it is technically possible to level some of these materials, especially magazines, it is not necessary. Given that anywhere from 5 to 30 percent of reading materials may need coding, and only if children are unable to self-select appropriate materials, it seems pointless. How do we color-code materials such as atlases and maps? It doesn't make sense. Websites are also difficult to level.

PART 4

Responses

Responses to Reading

Do I have to write another book report? Can't I just start reading another book?

Julie, Grade 3

Julie, I hear you loud and clear. When I was a child, the pleasures of reading were rewarding; however, having to write the dreaded book report at the end tarnished the entire experience. As I neared the end of a book, a dark cloud loomed overhead. The book report soured a perfectly pleasurable experience. I was also dismayed by the expectation that I had to respond to every book I read. The pure joy of reading was diminished to a less than pleasurable experience. Not surprisingly, children still feel this way. For teachers, the book report is often the pinnacle of what we use to access children's understandings of what they have read. The book report is our savior. It provides us with the accountability factor: Yes, I can prove the child has read and comprehended this book—look, he or she has written a book report!

If we examine what many children write when they complete a book report, we see that it is often a weak rendition of what actually happened. The basic plot is given and the piece is constructed with the usual phrases. "My favorite character was . . ." "The book was about . . ." "I like the part when . . ." Some children can even write reports without ever reading the book. Harrold, a third grader I met, had this down to a fine art. He read the blurb on the back cover, the chapter headings, and selected sections from different chapters. He also asked his friend who had already read the book to tell him what had happened. He used this knowledge to construct a book report that would lead you to believe he had actually read the book. He had mastered the art of deception but, to his credit, had a streak of ingenuity when it came to a painless way of writing a book report.

In looking at authentic responses to literature, we need to ask what makes sense when it comes to monitoring children's comprehension. A book report can be one method of achieving this goal, but we need to go beyond a general rendition of events, characters, or facts. Responses to literature need to be fueled by the learner's wonderings, surprises, and connections. Responses need to be driven by the reader's passion and not by a prescribed list of questions that becomes a blueprint for all responses.

How Often—and When—Do Students Respond?

The expectations for how often children should respond to their independent reading will vary from teacher to teacher and will depend on many factors. These include time constraints, teacher expectations, other curriculum programs, and district- and state-level assessment/testing schedules. What is important is that we don't expect our students to respond to everything they read. Although children need to know how to respond to their independent reading, it shouldn't dominate the reading workshop. We want our learners to spend most of their time reading, not just responding. Sometimes children may not be responding to their reading, and other times they may be completing responses each week. Children need to know how to respond as well as how to enjoy the reading experience. Students in older grades often need longer to respond than children in earlier grades because the texts they are reading are lengthier and more complex. Consequently, their responses tend to be more involved.

Concerning when students respond, I find it is necessary to allocate some class time. This can be part of reading workshop or at other designated times throughout the day. In the classrooms where I have worked, we always encouraged the children to work on their responses when they had completed other set tasks. Students can also work on their responses at home as part of homework.

Setting Up Responses Grades K–2

In establishing authentic ways for children to respond to their reading, remember that this is an ongoing process. They do not magically happen overnight, which was the case in Janet Mullins's grades one and two multiage classroom in Melbourne. First, we asked the children what they thought would be a good response to their reading. Typically, they responded with "write about it" or "draw a picture." Many children had no suggestions, as is often the case in kindergarten classrooms because of a lack of models. Janet and I needed to offer suggestions and construct a number of whole-class responses together based on a common text to explicitly demonstrate what a response looked like. We used some of our read-aloud and shared reading texts to help accomplish this goal. We also needed to demonstrate to the children how to respond to both fiction and nonfiction texts.

Janet and I commenced by reading Eric Carle's classic *The Very Hungry Caterpillar*. We then came up with a list of all the different ways we could respond to the text, as shown here. We found that most of the suggestions came from us because the children really had few ideas on how to effectively respond. Thinking aloud and modeling by the teacher is essential to giving children different examples of ways to respond and getting them to think of possibilities. Once Janet and I offered suggestions, many of the children began to think more divergently and offered wonderful suggestions.

Ways We Can Respond to *The Very Hungry Caterpillar*
- Draw different pictures of the hungry caterpillar as he grows into a butterfly.
- Write about how a caterpillar changes into a butterfly.
- Make a list of all the foods that are good to eat to make our bodies grow.
- Make a list of the foods that are not good for our bodies.
- Write and draw about our favorite parts of the story.

- Write and draw about anything we didn't like about the story.
- Make a model of the different stages the caterpillar goes through when changing into a butterfly.
- Tell the story to a friend.
- Make a tape of the story using our own words.
- Draw or paint a very hungry caterpillar eating leaves.
- Act out the hungry caterpillar growing into a caterpillar.

Once our list was constructed we selected one item from the list to construct a whole-class response. We listed all the foods that are good for our bodies. We also listed the foods that were good for very hungry caterpillars so that we could compare and contrast our nutritional needs with those of caterpillars. Janet and I had already agreed on this option before the whole-class demonstration so that we could have all the materials on hand. We showed the children pictures of foods we had cut out of magazines and discussed which foods are good for our bodies. We pasted these onto a chart, as seen in Figure 9.1. We then asked the children which foods were good for caterpillars and added these to the chart.

After the chart was completed, the children worked in pairs using large pieces of white paper, scissors, glue, and magazines to construct their own charts of foods that are good for our bodies and for caterpillars. These charts were displayed in the classroom. Janet's children were proud of their accomplishments and eager to produce responses to other literature introduced in read-aloud and shared reading encounters.

Figure 9.1
Chart Comparing Foods That Are Good for Our Bodies with That of *The Very Hungry Caterpillar*

Good Choice!

Ways to respond to our reading

- Write about your favorite part
- Make something to show what you have learned
- Talk to a friend about it.
- Act it out
- Put on a play
- Write about any connections you made
- Draw about it - Favorite part
  - Connections
  - Surprises
  - Amazing facts

Figure 9.2

Children's List of Ways to Respond to Their Reading

Over the following four weeks, Janet and I continued to do a response each week centered on both fiction and nonfiction texts introduced in whole-class settings. On each occasion, we made a list of the possible responses and then selected one to construct together. We gradually released responsibility to our learners by having each child select his or her own response from the generated list. For children who required additional support, we made suggestions and had them work in small-group settings. Then we brought the children together and made a master list of the different ways we could respond to our reading, as seen in Figure 9.2. We added to this list as we discovered additional ways to respond. Although we had used read-aloud and shared reading as the anchor for responding, it was now time for the children to apply this to their own independent reading. We invited them to find a text from their independent reading that they wanted to respond to and then to select a response from the master list. The expectations we placed on Janet's children were simple. They needed to respond to one piece of literature they read each week, unless other curriculum priorities took center stage.

Sharing Responses

Sharing our achievements is an important part of the learning process. It helps us validate what we have accomplished and our future endeavors. Arranging sharing opportunities in the classroom can be time-consuming. Having each child stand before the class to share his or her work can take time and may not be the most effective means of celebrating children's work. Children want to share their triumphs instantly and not wait a week until it is their turn to share.

To ensure what I term *instantaneous sharing*, Janet and I grouped the children into teams of three or four for small-group sharing sessions. We randomly grouped the children by pulling names out of a hat. We used one of the groups to demonstrate how to effectively share a piece in front of the class. We asked one of the team members to share his or her piece. We then began to model the types of questions we could ask and invited the other team members to do likewise. A list of these questions follows:

Questions You Could Ask

- Where did you get your idea?
- What do you like best about your response?
- How does your response show what happened in the story? (fiction)
- How does your response show what you learned from reading the book? (nonfiction)
- How would you make your response better next time?

We gave positive feedback to the team members when they raised questions. We encouraged them to listen to one another and always make eye contact. We also showed the children in the group how to take turns sharing. We then constructed a chart, as seen in Figure 9.3. We knew we needed to keep the chart simple and not overload the children with too much to think about. We didn't want the joys of sharing to be diminished by a complex set of procedures.

Once the children separated into groups to share, it was imperative to walk around the classroom and to provide additional support to each group. Although at first the children struggled to share their responses adequately, through repeated demonstrations, they soon became constructive thinkers, listeners, and talkers. This confirmed that children require multiple demonstrations and engagement before they internalize new learning.

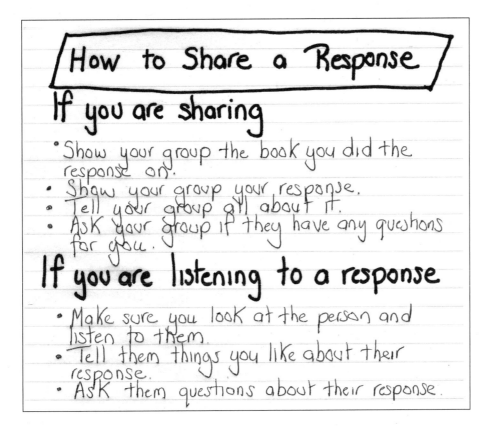

Figure 9.3
Chart Showing
Guidelines for Sharing

Ensuring Variety

Janet and I had ongoing, whole-class conversations with the children to ensure that they were selecting different ways to respond to their reading. We found that many of the children were becoming locked into doing the same type of response each week. We assisted them by giving each child a response log, as seen in Figure 9.4. This sheet can be filled out by the children or, in the case of kindergarten and early first grade, by the teacher. Refer to Appendix T for a blank version of this log. This record of responses helped both us and the children monitor selections to ensure variety. When we found that specific children were still responding in the same way even after whole-class mini-lessons, we used individual conferences as an anchor for further discussions and support. It was not long before Janet's children began responding in various and unique ways. Jala, a first grader, responded to her book about how to make salsa by going home and making some with her mother to bring in for the children to try. The salsa was a big hit, and the children told Jala that she should read more books about making things, especially food recipes. There was also a newfound interest in borrowing recipe books in the classroom and for a while they became the flavor of the week.

My Response Log

Name: Raffi Huk   Grade: 1

Date	Title	Response	Feelings
11/6	Building Things	Made a building with cardboard	😊
11/14	Going Fishing	Wrote about going fishing with Dad.	😊
11/21	Honey for Baby Bear	Drew picture of favorite part	😊
11/28	Zoo Looking	Designed his own zoo	😊
12/5	Snakes	Wrote/drew 5 most interesting facts	😊
12/13	Melting	Conducted an experiment	😐
12/20	Boats	Made a boat from cardboard	🙁
1/8	The Big Fat Worm	Retold story to a friend	😐
1/15	Dinosaurs, Dinosaurs	Drew/described favorite dinosaur	😊

😊 I am happy with my response.

😐 My response is okay.

🙁 My response could be better.

Figure 9.4
Raffi's Response Log

As seen in Figure 9.4, Janet and I decided to add a column that allowed the children to self-assess each response. I have always been a great believer in having children reflect on their endeavors. It allows them to decide how they can improve future works. Janet and I had conversations with the children about what the three smiley faces represented. Whenever children drew a sad face, we called them to conference to discuss ways that they could make sure their next response was one they were happy with.

Setting Up Responses Grades 3–6

As with setting up responses in the earlier grades, students in grades three through six also require careful scaffolding in how to respond to their reading. When I first introduced responses to Franca Paduano's third- and fourth-grade students in Melbourne, Australia, I was not surprised that writing a book report was their only suggestion. Like many intermediate learners, responding was a tedious task for them. The notion that responding to literature could be exciting and worthwhile was not something they had considered.

We began by discussing all the possible ways to respond to literature and listed the options on a chart. As with Janet's first- and second-grade students, Franca's students initially found it difficult to think of different possibilities, so we offered suggestions. We showed the students examples of responses from past years to give them ideas. To extend the students' thinking and initiate further discussions, we asked each student to bring the books bags that housed their independent reading selections. The students were put into small groups, and each group was

Good Choice!

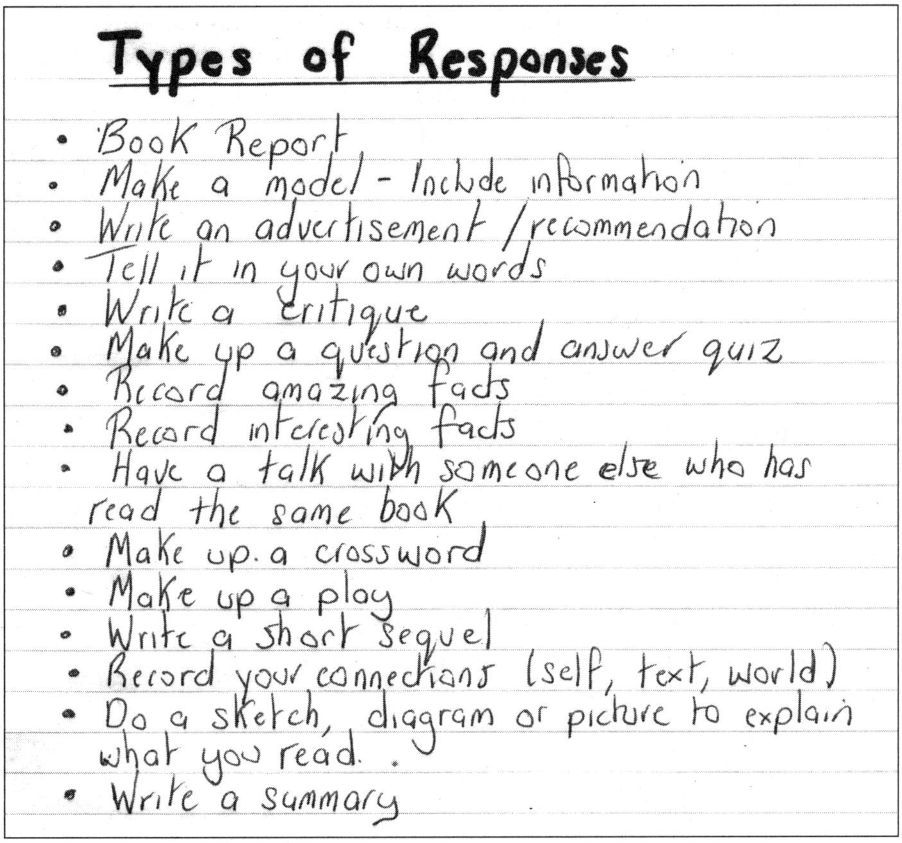

Figure 9.5
Chart Listing Possible
Responses

Types of Responses

- Book Report
- Make a model - Include information
- Write an advertisement /recommendation
- Tell it in your own words
- Write a critique
- Make up a question and answer quiz
- Record amazing facts
- Record interesting facts
- Have a talk with someone else who has read the same book
- Make up a crossword
- Make up a play
- Write a short sequel
- Record your connections (self, text, world)
- Do a sketch, diagram or picture to explain what you read.
- Write a summary

given a small piece of chart paper. We asked them to share the materials they were independently reading and discuss the different ways they could respond and then record these on the chart paper. This was an effective strategy, since it gave the students tangible pieces of literature to think about in a group setting rather than in isolation.

Responses are fueled by the material that has been read. Bringing students together and expecting them to know how to respond globally to literature is a difficult and unrealistic task. We brought the groups together to share their findings and then added these to our master chart, as shown in Figure 9.5. We were excited by the different options they came up with and so we asked them to select one of these and begin an individual response. Not surprisingly, none of the students opted to do a book report.

Franca and I gave the students up to two weeks to complete their initial responses, and we allowed them twenty minutes each day to work on these. We encouraged them to work on their responses after they had completed other set tasks and at home if time allowed. Janet and I ensured that when her students were working on responses in class we would offer support and suggestions. We were amazed at how important these responses became to the students. Every spare moment, they diligently added new thoughts to their responses. Their sense of pride was heartening. After they completed the responses, we grouped the students for a sharing session, similarly to how students were grouped in Janet's first- and second-grade classroom. We also needed to discuss effective ways to share responses and chart suggestions as shown here.

Suggestions for Sharing Responses

When You Are Sharing

- Make sure you are prepared. Have the text you responded to and your response ready.
- Keep you sharing to five minutes.
- Briefly tell your audience what the text is about.
- Tell your audience about why you chose to respond to the text in the way you did.
- Share what you liked most about your response.
- Share anything you would do differently if you were to do the response again.

When You Are Listening to Someone Share

- Make sure you look at the person.
- Listen to what they have to say.
- Tell them the things you liked best about their response.
- Ask them any questions you have about their response.

Providing Support

Over the next few months, Franca and I had to constantly provide whole-class demonstrations to strengthen the students' skills in producing and sharing a well-crafted response. Although the students' first efforts were commendable, we knew they needed time and continued support to better their efforts. A list of some of these demonstrations follows:

Demonstrations Provided

- Make sure the response gives important information and details about what you have just read.
- Ensure that responses are well presented.
- Use legible writing and drawings.
- Ensure variety in the way you respond.
- Make sure you respond to both fiction and nonfiction texts.
- Keep the responses simple and clear.
- Include enough information.

Figure 9.6
Luke's Response
Checklist

Name: Luke

What Makes a Good Response?

	Response 1	Response 2	Response 3	Response 4	Response 5	Response 6	Response 7	Response 8	Response 9
Name of Text									
Is my response colorful?	✓		✓	✓	✓			½	✓
Did I take time to complete this task?	✓		✓		✓	✓	✓		✓
Have I put in my best effort with this response?	✓	✓	✓	✓	✓	✓	✓	✓	✓
Does my response tell the reader about what I have learned?	✓	✓	✓	✓	✓	✓	✓	✓	
Have I included 5–10 amazing or important facts?		✓		✓		✓	✓	✓	
Am I proud of this book response?	✓		✓	½✓	✓	✓	✓	✓	✓
Have I used neat handwriting?	✓	✓	✓		✓	✓	✓	✓	✓
Is my drawing well designed?	✓		✓		✓				✓
Have I included enough information?	✓	✓	✓	✓		✓	✓		½
Have I checked my spelling?			✓		✓	✓	✓	✓	✓
Have I checked my punctuation?		✓	✓		✓		✓	✓	✓
Have I updated my reading response record sheet?	✓	✓	✓	✓	✓	✓	✓	✓	✓

- Check for spelling and punctuation.
- Learn how to share your response.
- Learn to ask questions of someone sharing a response.

At the conclusion of each demonstration, we asked the students whether their current responses needed revision based on the discussions. This led to the class's coming together to discuss the components of a good response. Franca and I charted their suggestions and created a checklist as shown in Figure 9.6. Refer to Appendix U for a copy of the checklist. This checklist was a valuable tool for showing the students the essential ingredients of a well-produced and well-presented response.

As seen in Figure 9.6, Luke had checked that the important features of each of his responses were included. For elements that are either not relevant to a particular response or not looked for, he left the space blank. His first response was about a novel; therefore, there was no need to include five to ten amazing facts, as this element was specific to nonfiction texts. Because this specific response was a visual representation, there was no need to check for spelling and punctuation. Luke came up with the measure "½." When I asked why he used this measure, he said that he was trying to be honest and had really only half-checked for these specific elements. I congratulated him on his honesty, and we shared his response sheet with the rest of the class. We had wonderful whole-class discussions on how sometimes because of time limits or other class work our responses may not always be as good as we would like them to be. Being sick or absent might also affect the quality of responses. The students realized that trying was important, that if they were unhappy with a particular response, then they should be honest and make sure their next response was better. Soon children were using the ½ measurement or, at times, "¼ " to signify that they were not totally satisfied with specific elements of their work.

Ensuring Variety

As with Janet's first- and second-grade students, Franca and I discovered that many students were locked into responding in selected ways. At first, most students wanted to use art and drama, preferring to do as little writing as possible. This was a result of book report fatigue. We needed to extend their responses to include written information about what they had read. We discussed with the students how writing could be incorporated into their responses. As with Janet's children, we provided them with a monitoring log, as seen in Figure 9.7. Refer to Appendix V for a copy. This sheet was not only valuable for self-monitoring the types of responses students completed, but also illustrated the specific text types they were reading. It assisted them in diversifying their selections to include a variety of genres. The response log also gave Franca and me wonderful springboards for discussions at both whole-class mini-lessons and individual conferences.

Before long, Franca's students were not only responding widely but with passion. I saw this passion for responses at its peak one day after many of the children had been reading about dolphins. Mario was appalled to discover that thousands of these magnificent creatures were

160

Figure 9.7
Mia's Response Log

My Response Log

Name Mia   Grade 3

Date	Title / Author	Text Type	Response
1/7	Superfudge Judy Blume	S	I drew a cartoon of the story
1/16	Ramona Quibly Beverly Cleary	S	I retold my favourite part
1/28	Should There Be Zoos Tony Stead	P	I wrote why I think there should be zoos
2/6	Meet Martin Luther King Jr James DeKay	B	I did a timeline of his life.
2/18	Everyday Science Experiments with Light Amy Merrill	P	I did some experiments
2/27	Green Sea Turtles Chris Blomquist	I	I wrote some amazing facts
3/10	Fearsome Femal Pirates Aileen Weintraub	B	Made wanted posters for them
3/19	The Village by the Sea Paula Fox	S	I wrote a review
4/1	Bud, Not Buddy Christopher Paul Curtis	S	I wrote about my connections

Text Type Key: B—Biography I—Informational P—Persuasive PR—Procedural
PO—Poem S—Story E—Explanation R—Retelling O—Other

killed each year by being caught in fishermen's nets. His response was immediate. He composed a letter to the Department of Wildlife and Fisheries informing them of his concern. Mario, who—like many other of his classmates—despised the dreaded book report, effortlessly composed this letter because it was driven by a passion to respond.

Ongoing Monitoring and Record-Keeping Grades K–6

By having students keep a response log, as previously discussed and shown in Figures 9.4 and 9.7, teachers can closely monitor the ways students respond to their reading. Teachers can guide students who are only responding in narrow ways. The response checklist shown in Figure 9.6 is also a valuable tool to assist students self-monitor and assess their achievements.

Besides response logs and checklists, keeping an assessment rubric for each child, as shown in Figure 9.8, is a valuable tool to monitor each student's progress and understandings. This rubric supplies an ongoing, overall picture of how each child is progressing when he or she responds to reading, and it is a useful tool for the teacher in providing both whole-class and individual guidance. Refer to Appendix W for a copy you may wish to use.

Figure 9.8
Assessment Rubric for Responses

Observation Rubric for Reading Responses Months of: November–January Child's Name: Raffi Huk Grade: One	Key: 1 Not in evidence 2 Showing signs of 3 Strengthening 4 Nearly always				
Date	11/6	11/21	12/13	1/8	1/22
Able to respond to a piece of fiction	3	3	3	4	4
Able to respond to a piece of nonfiction	2	2	3	3	3
Enjoys responding (attitude)	4	4	4	4	4
Is responding in different ways to information read	1	2	2	2	2
The information presented is clear and well organized	1	1	1	1	2
The response is neat and well presented	1	1	1	1	1
Key or important facts and events are presented in the response	2	2	2	2	2
Takes pride in responses	1	2	2	2	2
Able to share responses with peers	2	2	3	2	3
Able to reflect on ways to improve future responses	1	2	1	2	2

Additional Comments

Raffi needs to work on making his responses much clearer and organized. Tends to rush through everything in record speed. Loves responding. Always eager and engaged.

Responding Through Literature Circles/ Book Clubs

Literature circles and book clubs are a wonderful opportunity for a small group of students to read independently and to respond to a common text. They strengthen students' abilities to articulate thought by encouraging them to share their opinions with others in a safe setting. The establishment of literature circles and book clubs can promote healthy debates on a wide range of issues by encouraging students to listen to the opinions and thoughts of others. They provide opportunities for students to reflect on their own thinking and justify and modify existing thoughts based on the opinions of others.

The goal of literature circles or book clubs is to have students select their own materials, form their own groups, and initiate their own conversations about texts read. Harvey Daniels (2002) and Aidan Chambers (1996b) claim that ultimately the student needs to be in control, and therefore, these are really self-selected reading encounters, as discussed in Chapter 1. Although I agree, if students are to become ultimately responsible for choice, they require careful scaffolding by the teacher. Teacher support may include grouping students, providing books for them to read, helping students generate conversations by providing focused questions, and establishing roles within the group, as suggested by Daniels (2002), to ensure effective management and fluidity. I therefore initially view literature circles as teacher-directed or teacher-initiated encounters, as discussed in Chapter 2. When first established, literature circles are a bridge between guided reading and independent reading, and, ultimately, the student will become fully responsible for the process.

In *Book Talk: The Powers of Book Clubs in the Middle Grades* (2008), Anne Brailsford and Jan Coles give valuable scaffolds that the teacher can provide to lead students toward independence. *Literature Circles: Voices and Choice in Book Clubs and Reading Groups* by Harvey Daniels (2002) and *Tell Me: Children, Reading, and Talk* by Aidan Chambers (1996b) are also wonderful resources in how to establish and maintain effective literacy circles and book clubs.

Beginning Literature Circles and Book Clubs

When I introduce literature circles or book clubs to students, I begin with a specific book or a common text for the entire class to read. That way I can carefully model the process of working together in groups and the types of conversations that can be generated. Discussing a book can take up to two weeks, and I usually implement it as part of reading workshop. Because this is a small-group process, I use the time I would normally allocate for guided reading. Therefore, it is best to alternate between guided reading and literature circles/book clubs on a two-week cycle. The text I select needs to be one all my students can read independently. Struggling readers may need the book on tape or CD to provide additional support. When I select the text I also consider the book's content. It needs to be a book that will interest my students and raise issues they can connect with.

After I select a book, I gather the students together and inform them that we will be reading and discussing a particular title in both small groups and as a whole class. I tell them that in time they will become responsible for selecting their own books and forming their own groups. By being informed of my goals, my learners are better able to understand the importance of our working together on one book before they go it alone. I read the first chapter of the book to the students and have them follow along in their own copies. This creates a sense of community and is a great way to immerse them in the story.

After reading the first chapter, I divide the students into groups of three or four. When grouping the students, I take into account any student dynamics. I need to ensure that one group does not consist of students who have trouble staying on task. I give each group an organizer to initiate discussions. The organizer is divided into four sections, as explained in Figure 9.9. Refer to Appendix X for a copy of the organizer. The organizer is based on work by Aidan Chambers from *Tell Me: Children, Reading, and Talk* (1996b). Before sending the students to their discussion groups, I advise them to use the four-section organizer to generate discussions. I appoint a scribe for each group to record the key points under each of the categories on the organizer. It is beneficial to have each student take turns within the group to discuss one major

Figure 9.9
Organizer for Literature Circle and Book Club Discussions

Likes	Dislikes	Puzzles	Connections
Students record what they like about the chapters read so far. These elements may include characters, plot, issues raised, the author's writing style, voice, and illustrations.	Students record what they disliked about the chapters read so far. These elements may include characters, plot, issues raised, the author's writing style, voice, and illustrations.	Students record questions they have about the setting, plot, characters, and author's craft.	Students record connections they made. These may include connections with self, other texts, and the world.

Good Choice!

like, dislike, puzzle, and connection. In this way, all students get a chance to talk. I inform the students that if their like, dislike, puzzle, or connection is mentioned by other group members, then the scribe should put a checkmark next to it on the organizer to indicate the number of group members who had similar thoughts. While the students are engaged in these discussions, I walk around the classroom giving support as needed.

Once that is completed, I bring the students together and record each group's responses on a large chart that is divided into the four categories. The students have an opportunity to independently read the next chapter and engage in conversations using the organizer as an anchor. I again bring the groups together and record their key points on the large, whole-class organizer. I repeat this process until the book is finished.

Releasing Responsibility to the Students

When students have been through the whole-class experience, I gradually release responsibility to them. I'll have multiple copies of five or six books and ask each student to select two they are interested in reading. I give them a piece of paper and ask them to write their names and their two choices. I then use these to form groups. When forming the groups, I consider group dynamics and students' abilities to read the books they have chosen. I try to limit the groups to five students each. If I have more than ten copies of a selected text, sometimes two groups may be reading the same book. I give the groups opportunities to meet daily and use the organizer to record thoughts. Often I ask the students to read selected chapters at home so that when they do meet they are engaged in conversations.

My final step is to have the students form their own groups based on the text they each want to read and respond to. To provide support, I supply multiple copies of texts for them to select. This is the most challenging phase in setting up literature circles/book clubs because the students need to not only be responsible for forming groups but able to select a text that all members can read. Students want to work with their friends, and we end up with separate groups of boys and girls. Students who don't always work effectively together seem to form groups with one another. To help alleviate these challenges, it is essential to have conversations with students and provide ground rules for forming groups. When I worked in Peter's fifth-grade classroom, we came up with a set of guidelines. If the students consistently broke these rules, then they forfeited the right to choose their own groups.

Guidelines for Forming Literature/Book Clubs

- No group should have more than six members.
- If you see someone who is not in a group, invite them to join you.
- Each group must have at least two boys and two girls.
- Try to work with people you haven't worked with before.
- If you have worked with the same person two times before, then you need to be in a different group.
- The group should vote on which text to read.
- Happily accept the decision of the group.
- Each member must be able to read the text selected. If not, another text should be chosen.
- When you meet together, always take turns speaking.
- Always listen to what others have to say and make eye contact with them.
- Encourage and give positive feedback to your group members.

Figure 9.10
Meg's Literature Circle/Book Club Evaluation Sheet

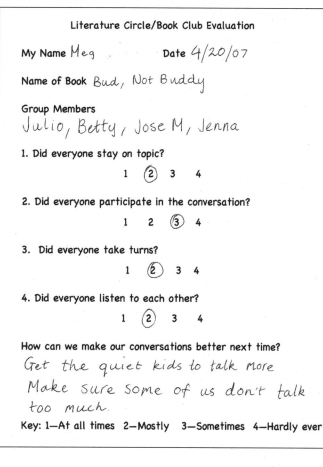

Literature Circle/Book Club Evaluation

My Name Meg   Date 4/20/07

Name of Book Bud, Not Buddy

Group Members
Julio, Betty, Jose M, Jenna

1. Did everyone stay on topic?
    1 ② 3 4

2. Did everyone participate in the conversation?
    1 2 ③ 4

3. Did everyone take turns?
    1 ② 3 4

4. Did everyone listen to each other?
    1 ② 3 4

How can we make our conversations better next time?
Get the quiet kids to talk more
Make sure some of us don't talk
too much.

Key: 1—At all times 2—Mostly 3—Sometimes 4—Hardly ever

Ongoing Monitoring and Assessment

Literature circles revolve around students' ability to respond to their reading through common talk; therefore, it is essential that students are able to self-monitor these conversations. Giving each group a "Literature Circle/ Book Club Evaluation Sheet," as seen in Figure 9.10, is a useful way to achieve this goal. Refer to Appendix Y for a copy. I first got this idea when I worked with Judy Ballester in her fifth-grade classroom in Queens, New York. I give each student in the group a copy of the monitoring sheet to fill out after they have engaged in their book talk conversations. After they've completed the sheet, I ask the group to come together to share their findings. The students have to justify to one another why they circled each number and come to some kind of consensus. I encourage them to use their findings to ensure greater cooperation at their next meeting.

Good Choice!

In addition to students' assessing their own endeavors to work together cooperatively in responding to a common text, it is helpful to keep track of each student's progress. To accomplish this, I use an assessment rubric as seen in Figure 9.11. Refer to Appendix Z for a copy. This rubric allows me to monitor each student's progress and to provide whole-class and small-group demonstrations based on common needs.

Figure 9.11
Assessment Rubric for Literature Circles/Book Clubs

Observation Rubric for Literature Circles/Book Clubs	**Key:**				
Months of: March/April	**1 Not in evidence**				
Student's Name: Julio Ramos	**2 Showing signs of**				
Grade: 5	**3 Strengthening**				
Independent Reading Level: S/T	**4 Nearly always**				

Date	3/8	3/15	3/22	3/29	4/7
Able to work cooperatively with other members	3	3	3	3	4
Able to express opinions	2	2	2	2	3
Can listen to others thinking without interrupting	4	4	4	4	4
Able to engage in discussions with informational texts (nonfiction)	2	3	2	2	3
Able to engage in discussions with stories/novels (fiction)	3	3	3	3	3
Accepts others' opinions even when they differ from his or her own	2	2	3	2	3
Can take on specific role within the group	4	4	4	4	4
Able to use illustrative sources such as illustrations, graphs, and maps to initiate discussion	1	2	2	2	2
Is aware that his or her thinking may be biased	1	1	1	2	2
Stays on track during discussions	2	2	2	2	2
Makes eye contact with others when speaking and listening	3	3	4	4	4
Able to disagree in a constructive manner without getting personal	2	2	2	2	3

Additional Comments
More experiences needed in working with illustrative sources. Still going off track during discussions. Other group members value his input.

Resources for Responding

There are literally hundreds of options when it comes to the ways that students can respond to their reading, and in this final chapter I show you a few examples. Figure 10.1 lists several possibilities based on the text type. I have also included a number of graphic organizers in this chapter because they can provide invaluable support to children as they develop their responses. So many authentic and engaging alternatives to the dreaded book report exist, and I'm sure your students will come up with many more!

Text Type	Possible Responses
Procedural such as recipes, directions, and maps	■ Explain in your own words how to make the item to a friend or family member ■ Actually make or construct the item ■ Construct your own map/directions ■ Make a cookbook of your favorite recipes ■ Keep a journal
Informational/descriptive material about animals, plants, space, transport	■ Write a question-and-answer pamphlet ■ List the ten most amazing facts you found ■ Create a chart or poster of the facts you found most interesting ■ Record information onto a cassette tape for others to listen to ■ Create a video of yourself talking about what you discovered ■ Produce a mini-documentary ■ Write a true-or-false sheet ■ Design a questionnaire ■ Make a mobile ■ Create a brochure ■ Make a three-dimensional model
Informational/descriptive material about places	■ Create an advertising brochure on the place ■ Write a brief travel guide ■ Produce a mini-documentary ■ Create a true-or-false questionnaire about the place ■ Write the ten most amazing facts
Biographies/Autobiographies	■ Draw a portrait of the person ■ Write a short biography about a friend or family member ■ Write an autobiography ■ List the most important things about the person you read about ■ Create a wanted poster ■ Make a time line of the person's life
Poetry	■ Make up your own poem ■ Begin a book of your favorite poems ■ Record your favorite poems on a cassette or CD for others to hear ■ Create a picture to represent what the poem was about ■ Make a model to represent the poem

Figure 10.1
Possible Responses
Based on Text Types
Read

Text Type	Possible Responses

Stories/Novels	■ Write a book report
	■ Talk to someone else who has read the book
	■ Write, draw, or talk about:
	  ■ connections you made (self, text, world)
	  ■ most exciting part
	  ■ parts that made you sad
	  ■ parts that made you laugh
	  ■ characters you liked or disliked
	  ■ anything that amazed you
	  ■ parts you didn't like
	  ■ parts that scared you
	  ■ wonderings you had
	■ Put on a short performance of the story
	■ Create a cartoon of the events
	■ Write a short script of the story
	■ Write a review
	■ Draw a portrait of your favorite character
	■ Design a new cover for the book
	■ Write a recommendation
	■ Retell the events as a cartoon

Persuasive	■ Hold a debate ■ Write letters to a newspaper ■ Write letters to people in the community ■ Write a review ■ Make advertisement posters to be displayed around the school or in the local community ■ Conduct an interview
Explanations/How and Why	■ Conduct an experiment for your classmates to explain a specific phenomenon ■ Create a chart or poster to explain a phenomenon ■ Explain the phenomenon to a friend
Retelling of historical and/or important events	■ Make a time line using words ■ Make a time line using pictures ■ Make a time line using words and pictures ■ Write a summary of the events that happened ■ Represent what happened through pictures with labels

Figure 10.1
Possible Responses
Based on Text Types
Read *(continued)*

Example of Responses

Jason Shao
Title Origami   Date 24-10-06
Response Number 1~5

Subject: Origami
Type: Pinwheel
Instructions:

1.
2.
3.
4.
5.
6.
7.

Figure 10.2 How to Make a Pinwheel

Title Judy Moody Gets Famous!   Date 31/5/06
Response Number 3

This story was about...
Judy's everyday moods.

About Judy
Name: Judy Moody   Pet: Mouse (a cat)
Best Friend: Rocky   Brother: Stink
What she wants: To be famous   Her enemy friend: Jessica Finch

Judy Moody
Rocky
Stink
Jessica Finch
Mouse

Figure 10.4 A Character Profile—Grade 3

Figure 10.3
Writing up an
Experiment—Grade 2

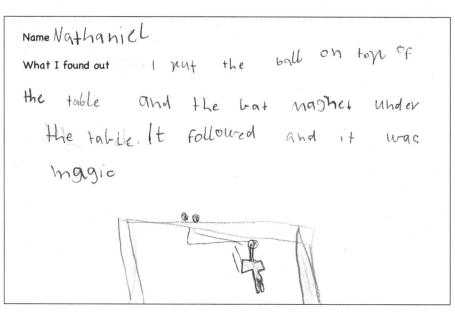

Name Nathaniel

What I found out   I put the ball on top of
the table and the bat magnet under
the table. It followed and it was
magic

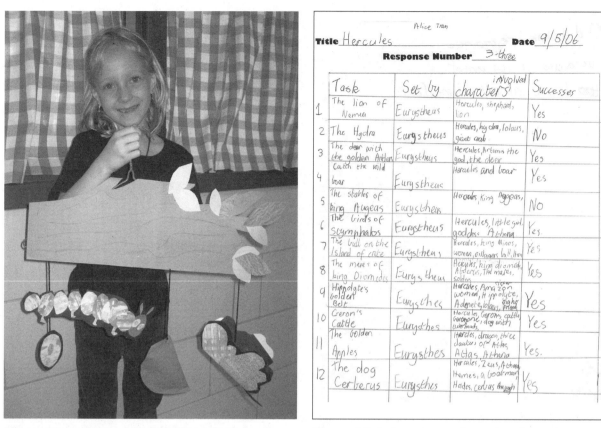

Figure 10.5 Making a Mobile of the Life Cycle of a Caterpillar—Grade 1

Figure 10.6 Documenting the Battles of Hercules—Grade 6

The handwritten form in Figure 10.6 reads:

Alice Tran

Title Hercules   **Date** 9/5/06

Response Number 3-three

	Task	Set by	Involved characters	Successes
1	The lion of Nemea	Eurystheus	Hercules, shephaed, lion	Yes
2	The Hydra	Eurystheus	Hercules, hydra, Iolaus, giant crab	No
3	The deer with the golden Antlers	Eurystheus	Hercules, Artemis the god, the deer	Yes
4	Catch the wild boar	Eurystheus	Heracles and boar	Yes
5	The stables of King Augeas	Eurystheus	Hercules, King Augeas,	No
6	The birds of Stymphalos	Eurystheus	Hercules, little girl, goddess Athena	Yes
7	The bull on the Island of crete	Eurystheus	Hercules, king Minos, women, villagers bull, Iton	Yes
8	The mares of king Diomedes	Eurystheus	Hercules, king diomedes, Abderus, the mares, soldien	Yes
9	Hippolyte's Golden Belt	Eurysthes	Hercules, Amazon women, Hippolyte, Admete, Iolaus, Eight	Yes
10	Geron's Cattle	Eurysthes	Hercules, Geron, cattle, Gorgogne, dog with two heads	Yes
11	The Golden Apples	Eurysthes	Hercules, dragon, three daughters of Atlas, Atlas, Athena	Yes.
12	The dog Cerberus	Eurysthes	Hercules, 2 eus, Athena, Hermes, a boatman Hades, cerbus through	Yes

Figure 10.7 Model and Information About Stonehenge—Grade 3

Figure 10.8
Outside of a Brochure on Pandas Written in Spanish—Grade 3

Figure 10.9
Inside of a Brochure on Pandas Written in Spanish—Grade 3

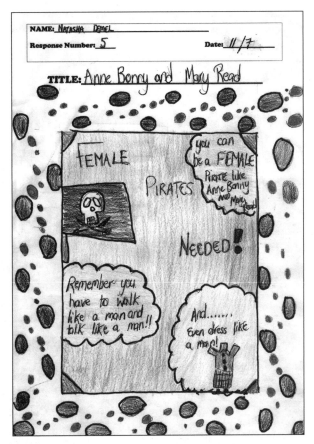

Title Electrical Storms	Date 1/6/06
Response Number 2	
Ribbon lightning	Bead lighting
•appers side-by-side	lightning that changes
•not rare	to look like a string
•looks like stripes	of beads
•looks like a ribbon	•not rare
or tie men wear	•after chages to string
at speciel ocations.	of beads then fades.
Ball lightning	fork lightning
•only lasts for a	•most seen lightning
second	•not rare
•rarest lightning.	•appers to have diffrent
•looks like a floating	braches.
soft ball in the	•looks like a forke
sk...	too.

Figure 10.10 Comparisons of Different Types of Electrical Storms—Grade 5

Figure 10.11 Advertisement for Female Pirates—Grade 2

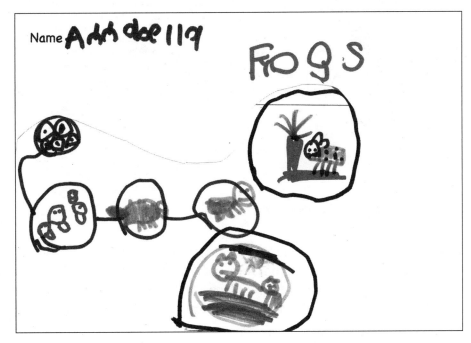

Figure 10.12
A Drawing of the Life Cycle of a Frog—Kindergarten

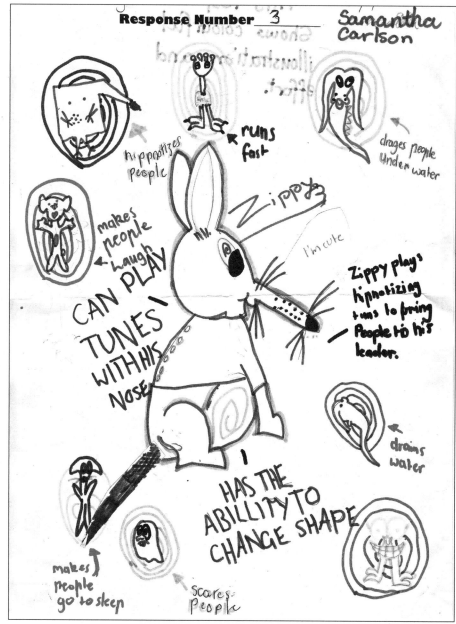

Using Organizers

Organizers are a helpful means to give children a structure for responding. It is essential that these organizers are first explored in a whole-class setting before students use them independently. In this way, they will know how to best use these when independently responding to a selected text.

Animal Facts

Name: _____ **Date:** _____

Animal	Habitat	Body Covering	Food	Predators

Amazing Facts I Learned About

Name: _____ **Grade:** _____

The best thing I found out

Other Great Facts

Good Choice!

How to Make _____

Name: _____ **Grade:** _____

This is what you need

These are the steps

My Map of _____

Name: _____ **Grade:** _____

Good Choice! Supporting Independent Reading and Response K–6 by Tony Stead. Copyright © 2008. Stenhouse Publishers.

Biography on _____

Name: _____ **Grade:** _____

Good Choice! Supporting Independent Reading and Response K–6 by Tony Stead. Copyright © 2008. Stenhouse Publishers.

Key details about birth and growing up

Key accomplishments—What made them famous

Biography on _____

Name: _____ **Grade:** _____

Connections you made

Review: What did you think about this text?

My Portrait of _____

Name: _____ **Grade:** _____

Title

Name: _____ **Grade:** _____

Name of text/book Number	Response

Good Choice! Supporting Independent Reading and Response K–6 by Tony Stead. Copyright © 2008. Stenhouse Publishers.

Chart Showing Cause and Effect

Name: _____ **Grade:** _____

Title of Book: _____

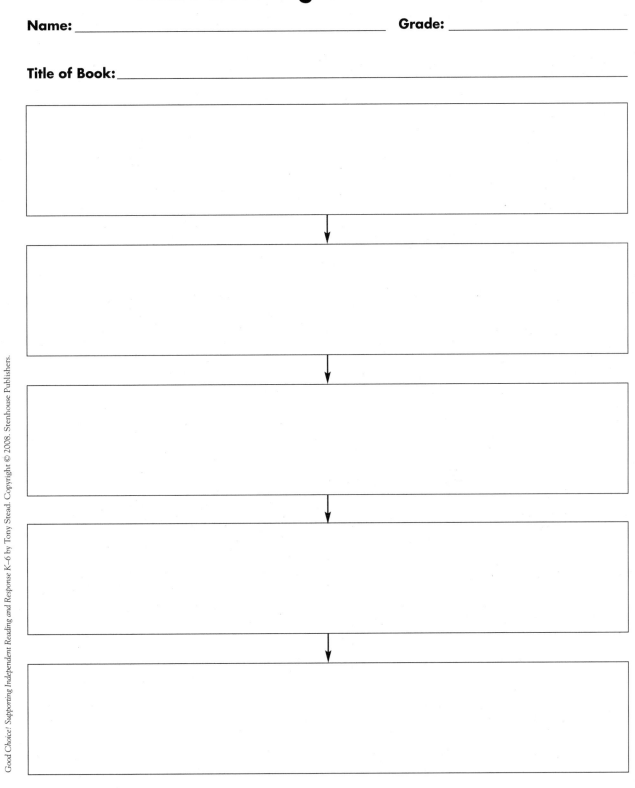

My Cartoon of Events

Name: _____ **Grade:** _____

Title of Book: _____

Good Choice! Supporting Independent Reading and Response K–6 by Tony Stead. Copyright © 2008. Stenhouse Publishers.

Good Choice!

Good Choice! Supporting Independent Reading and Response K–6 by Tony Stead. Copyright © 2008. Stenhouse Publishers.

Title

Name: _____ Grade: _____

Title of Book or Article: _____

These are the best facts presented	These are the main opinions presented	This is how strong I thought the article was

Character Analysis

Name: _____ Grade: _____

Title of Book: _____

Likes	**Best friends**	**Dislikes**
Best qualities	**What I think about them**	**Worst qualities**

Good Choice! Supporting Independent Reading and Response K–6 by Tony Stead. Copyright © 2008. Stenhouse Publishers.

Good Choice!

Time Line

Name: _____ **Grade:** _____

Title of Book: _____

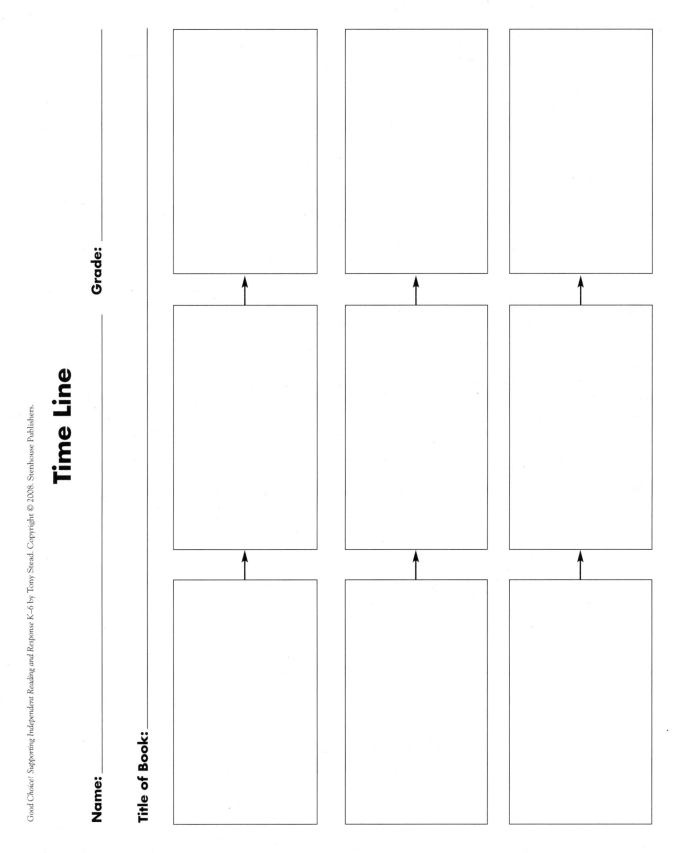

Comparing Characters

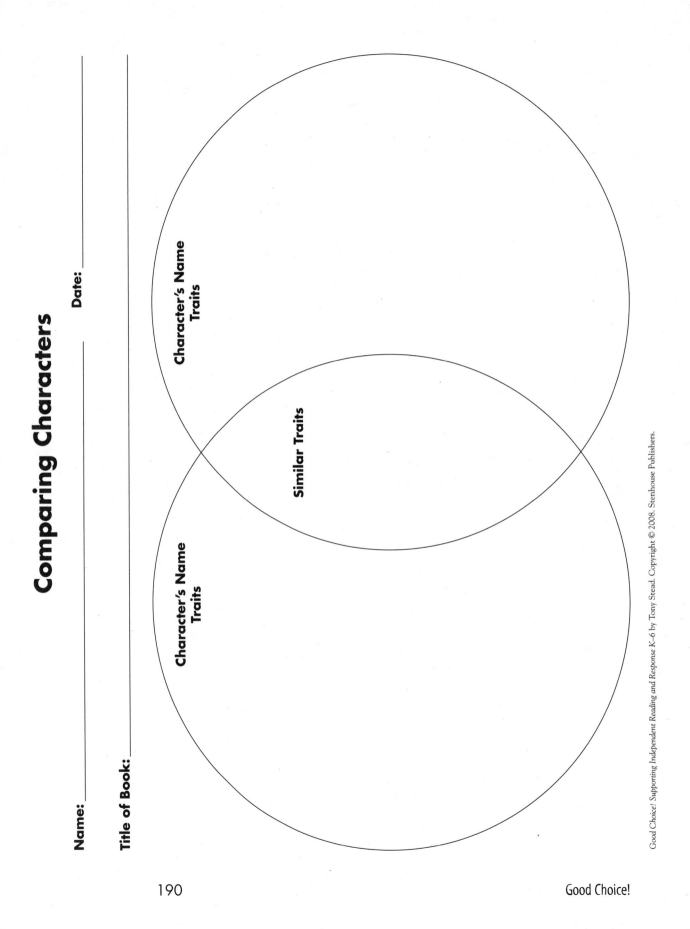

Character's Name
Traits

Similar Traits

Character's Name
Traits

Good Choice! Supporting Independent Reading and Response K–6 by Tony Stead. Copyright © 2008. Stenhouse Publishers.

Animal Brochure (Outside)

Outside template for brochure on a specific animal. *Note:* Photocopy outside and inside templates back to back, then fold to make a brochure.

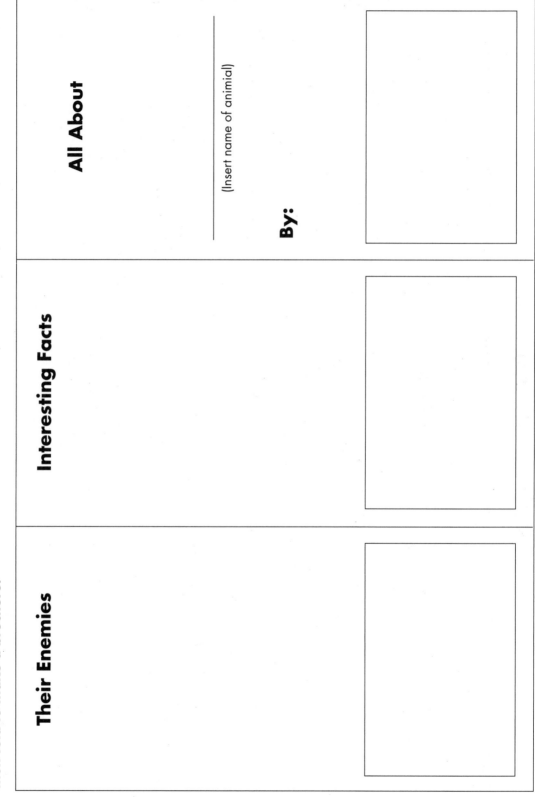

Their Enemies

Interesting Facts

All About

_____
(Insert name of animial)

By:

Animal Brochure (Inside)

Inside template for brochure on a specific animal. *Note:* **Photocopy outside and inside templates back to back, then fold to make a brochure.**

Appearance

Habitat

What They Eat

Good Choice! Supporting Independent Reading and Response K–6 by Tony Stead. Copyright © 2008. Stenhouse Publishers.

Place Brochure (Outside)

Outside template for brochure on a specific place. *Note:* Photocopy outside and inside templates back to back, then fold to make a brochure.

Shopping

Climate

Come and Visit

_____

(Insert name of place)

By:

Place Brochure (Inside)

Inside template for brochure on a specific place. *Note:* Photocopy outside and inside templates back to back, then fold to make a brochure.

Things to Do	Things to See	Food to Eat

Appendixes

A. Book Changing Schedule
B. Reading Log
C. Log of Books and Magazines Recommended
D. Reading Log for Beginning and Early Readers
E. Brochure for Parents K–2 (Outside and Inside)
F. Brochure for Parents 3–5 (Outside and Inside)
G. About Me
H. Organizer for Author Study
I. RAN Organizer
J. Survey of Interests
K. Survey of Interests for Early Readers
L. About the Author
M. Organizer for Locating and Recording Specific Information
N. RAN Organizer
O. RAN Organizer for Kindergarten and First Grade
P. Organizer for Student Reflection on Selecting
    Appropriate Texts
Q. Teacher's Conference Record Sheet
R. Observation Rubric for Independent Reading
S. Student's Individual Goals
T. Response Log for Children in Early Grades
U. Response Checklist
V. Response Log for Children in Grades 3–6
W. Observation Rubric for Reading Responses
X. Organizer for Literature Circle and Book Club Discussions
Y. Literature Circle/Book Club Evaluation
Z. Assessment Rubric for Literature Circles/Book Clubs

Appendix A: Book Changing Schedule

Monday	Tuesday	Wednesday	Thursday	Friday

Appendix B: Reading Log

Name: _____ Grade:_____

Title _____

Author _____

Date _____ **Genre** _____

Title _____

Author _____

Date _____ **Genre** _____

Title _____

Author _____

Date _____ **Genre** _____

Title _____

Author _____

Date _____ **Genre** _____

Title _____

Author _____

Date _____ **Genre** _____

Title _____

Author _____

Date _____ **Genre** _____

Title _____

Author _____

Date _____ **Genre** _____

Nonfiction

B—Biography

H—How To

D—Description/Explanation

P—Persuasive

R—Retelling (Historical)

NO—Other

Fiction

F—Fantasy

M—Mystery

HF—Historical Fiction

RF—Realistic Fiction

A—Adventure

SF—Science Fiction

FO—Other

Star Rating

   *   Don't Bother

  **   Okay

 *** Really Good

**** A Real Winner

Appendix C: Log of Books and Magazines Recommended

Name: _____ **Grade:** _____

Books and Magazines I Want to Read		
Name of book/magazine	**Author**	**Recommended by**

Good Choice! Supporting Independent Reading and Response K–6 by Tony Stead. Copyright © 2008. Stenhouse Publishers.

Appendix D: Reading Log for Beginning and Early Readers

Name: _____ **Grade:** _____

Title _____ **Date** _____ **Level** _____

Title _____ **Date** _____ **Level** _____

Title _____ **Date** _____ **Level** _____

Title _____ **Date** _____ **Level** _____

Title _____ **Date** _____ **Level** _____

Title _____ **Date** _____ **Level** _____

Title _____ **Date** _____ **Level** _____

Title _____ **Date** _____ **Level** _____

Title _____ **Date** _____ **Level** _____

Title _____ **Date** _____ **Level** _____

Title _____ **Date** _____ **Level** _____

Title _____ **Date** _____ **Level** _____

Title _____ **Date** _____ **Level** _____

Title _____ **Date** _____ **Level** _____

Title _____ **Date** _____ **Level** _____

Title _____ **Date** _____ **Level** _____

Title _____ **Date** _____ **Level** _____

Key: N—Nonfiction   F—Fiction

Appendix E: Brochure for Parents K–2 (Outside)

Selecting Texts

- What makes a good book is your child's reaction to it!
- Look for books that:
  - Rhyme
  - Have predictable stories and repeated phrases
  - Have colorful illustrations
  - Extend personal experiences

Common Concerns

The book my child brings home is

- too easy—this is fine because they need to feel successful
- too hard—great, read it to them and enjoy it
- had it before—familiar reads are helpful with comprehension, fluency, and phrasing and have a genuine place in learning to read

Supporting Your Child

- Read to your child every day.
- Find a comfortable place to read.
- Reading aloud helps children expand their vocabulary, appreciate the value of books and other texts, understand new ideas and concepts, and learn about the world around them.
- Encourage your child to have a go at reading and praise all attempts.
- Talk about the characters, people, and events and encourage your child to express their opinions about books.

Reading at Home

A Guide for Parents

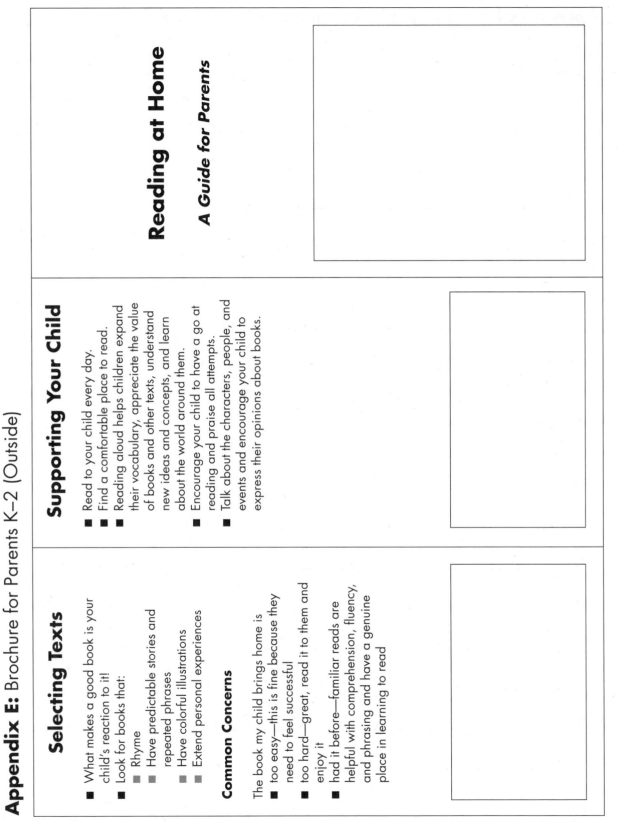

Good Choice! Supporting Independent Reading and Response K–6 by Tony Stead. Copyright © 2008. Stenhouse Publishers.

Good Choice! Supporting Independent Reading and Response K–6 by Tony Stead. Copyright © 2008. Stenhouse Publishers.

Appendix E: Brochure for Parents K–2 (Inside)

Reading to and with Your Child

Before Reading

■ Allow your child to select the book and discuss the reasons for the selection.
■ Encourage your child to look at the title and cover of a book and talk about what it might be about.

During Reading

■ If your child is a beginning reader, sometimes it's good to follow the words with your finger.
■ Ask questions: *What is happening now? What do you think will happen next? Why is he or she doing that?*
■ Answer your child's questions even if it interrupts the flow of the story.
■ Encourage your child to look at the pictures for clues for the story or unknown words.
■ Put the book away if your child has lost interest.
■ If your child wants to read it, let him or her and never dwell on mistakes!

After Reading

■ Talk about the book—characters, pictures, plots, and settings.
■ Discuss what was learned if it was a nonfiction book.
■ Compare the people and events in books with those in real life.

What to Read at Home

■ Anything and everything
■ Newspapers
■ TV guides
■ Recipe books
■ Emails
■ Great literature that you love
■ Local library books
■ Books from school
■ Information from websites

Developing Concepts About Print

If your child is just learning how to read:

Select one or two items from the following list to point out and discuss with your child each time you read together:

■ Front and back of the book
■ Right way up
■ Books are read from front to back
■ Pages are turned to reveal the next part of the book
■ A page is read from left to right and top to bottom
■ Print is different from pictures. Point to the print as you read
■ Pictures support the print
■ Talk about letters, sounds, words, and sentences
■ Numbers and letters are different
■ Letters have two forms—capital and lowercase

Reading at Home

A Guide for Parents

How to Support Your Child

- Read to or with your child regularly or let him or her read to you.
- Expose your child to a wide variety of texts and give encouragement to read new material.
- Encourage your child to talk about how characters or people are presented in texts, and make comparisons with real life.
- Talk about plots, settings, characters, events, information.
- Encourage your child to express and justify his or her reactions to the texts he or she read.
- Point out and discuss words that you think your child will not understand.
- Talk about how to find information in different texts, e.g., using the index, looking for headings.

Helping with Research

- This means guiding, advising, and talking things through.
- Ensure that the final product reflects your child's individual effort and design.
- If you feel tempted to do the research yourself, ask, "Will this help my child to learn?"
- Remember it's not your homework!!!!

What Can You Do?

- Suggest topics or focus.
- Help with locating information—library, book stores, family outing to museum/gallery, emailing someone, browsing the Web and downloading.
- Have your child discuss the topic and jot down ideas or questions before he or she starts researching.
- Discuss whether the information found is relevant to the child's study.
- Help your child group and organize information.
- Encourage your child to use the following procedure when taking notes:
  - Short notes—jot down key words and phrases with the reference material open
  - Long notes—close the reference material and use the short note to make sentences

Good Choice! Supporting Independent Reading and Response K–6 by Tony Stead. Copyright © 2008. Stenhouse Publishers.

Appendix F: Brochure for Parents 3–5 (Inside)

Reading with Your Child

Your children may prefer to read texts themselves. However, if they still enjoy being read to, then make time to continue doing this. Continue to vary the type of texts that you read to them, e.g., science fiction, mystery, and nonfiction.

When reading to your child, consider any of the following:

- Allow your child to select the text and discuss the reasons for the selection.
- Discuss what you both think the text might be about.
- If you are reading a text as a serial, talk about what has happened so far and ask questions.
- Throughout the reading sometimes stop and ask questions.
- Allow your child to raise questions even if it interrupts the reading.
- Put aside a text if your child has lost interest.

During or After Reading

- Discuss characters, plot, setting, and events.
- Discuss what was learned from informational texts.
- Compare characters and events in the texts with real-life people.
- Compare the texts with other texts read.
- Catch your child's attention by reading a small part of a text or the first chapter then allowing the child to finish reading the book independently.
- Whenever there is time available, discuss what is being read and what is being enjoyed.
- Read some books that you enjoy so they see that you also love reading.
- Provide sticky notes for your child to flag areas they would like to discuss after the reading.

Types of Texts

- Library books
- Books from school
- Books that are now films or videos
- Newspapers
- Recipe books
- Magazines, comics, dictionaries, street directories, atlases
- Favorite authors
- CD-ROMs and websites of book publishers
- Information from websites

Supporting Comprehension

Different types of questions and involvement in discussions will allow your child to respond to texts, build concepts, clarify meaning, explore issues, share perspectives, form opinions, and refine thinking.

Appendix G: About Me

Name: _____	**Grade:** _____

I was born in

In my family there is

My favorite hobbies are

My favorite foods are

When I grow up I want to be

My favorite color is

The book I like the most is

I like these sports

My favorite movie is

Appendix H: Organizer for Author Study

My Name: _____   **Name of Author:** _____

Biographical Details	**About the Illustrations**
Messages in Their Stories	**What I Like**
Author Craft	**My Connections**

Appendix I: RAN Organizer

Name: _____   Grade: _____

Facts About:

Facts I Think I Know	Facts Confirmed	New Facts I Learned

Appendix J: Survey of Interests

Name: _____			Grade: _____		

Put an X next to your favorite topics.

Animals		Insects		Space	
Dinosaurs		Sports		Reptiles	
The Sea		The Ocean		Countries	
Experiments		Making Things		Famous People	
Adventure Stories		Science Fiction		Mysteries	
Weather		Plants		Scary Stories	
Birds		Sports Biographies		Music	
Creepy Crawlies		Legends		Fables	
Games and Puzzles		Fairy Tales		Food	

What other topics do you like to read about?

Good Choice! Supporting Independent Reading and Response K–6 by Tony Stead. Copyright © 2008. Stenhouse Publishers.

Appendix K: Survey of Interests for Early Readers

Name: _____ **Grade:** _____

Draw the things you like to read about.

Good Choice! Supporting Independent Reading and Response K–6 by Tony Stead. Copyright © 2008. Stenhouse Publishers.

Appendix K

Appendix L: About the Author

Name: _____ **Grade:** _____

About Me

Other Publications

Appendix M: Organizer for Locating and Recording Specific Information

Name: _____ Grade: _____

These animals live in deserts.	**These animals live in the ocean.**	**These animals live in fresh water.**
These animals live in trees.	**These animals live in jungles.**	**These animals live in forests.**
These animals live under the ground.	**These animals live where there's snow.**	**These animals live in mountains.**

Good Choice! Supporting Independent Reading and Response K–6 by Tony Stead. Copyright © 2008. Stenhouse Publishers.

Appendix N: RAN Organizer

Name: _____ Grade: _____

Topic: _____ Website(s): _____

Content	What I Think I Know	C	M	New Facts	Wonderings
Food/Diet					
Appearance					
Habitat					

Key: C—confirmed information   M—misconceptions   O—other websites

Appendix O: RAN Organizer for Kindergarten and First Grade

Name: _____ Topic: _____

What I think I know about

New facts I learned

Appendix P: Organizer for Student Reflection on Selecting Appropriate Texts

Name: _____ Grade: _____

These are the strategies I use to select a suitable text.

Good Choice! Supporting Independent Reading and Response K–6 by Tony Stead. Copyright © 2008. Stenhouse Publishers.

Appendix Q: Teacher's Conference Record Sheet

| Name: _____ | Grade: _____ |

Date	Conference Notes

Appendix R: Observation Rubric for Independent Reading

Observation Rubric for Independent Reading Months of: Child's Name: Grade: Independent Reading Level:	Key: 1 Not in evidence 2 Showing signs of 3 Strengthening 4 Nearly always				
Date					
Selects fiction texts for independent reading					
Selects nonfiction texts for independent reading					
Able to select fiction material at appropriate readability levels					
Able to select nonfiction material at appropriate readability levels					
Reads widely with fiction, e.g., fantasy, fables, adventures, mysteries, science fiction, realistic fiction					
Reads widely with nonfiction, e.g., biographies, magazines, maps, articles, descriptions, procedures, persuasions					
Can talk about information read					
Has built up stamina for independently reading fiction					
Has built up stamina for independently reading nonfiction					
Reads with fluency					
Reads with expression					
Able to gain information from pictures and photographs					
Able to interpret information from illustrative sources such as tables, graphs, and maps					
Uses strategies to work out the meaning of unknown words					

Additional Comments

Appendix S: Student's Individual Goals

Name:	Grade:

Date	Goals to Work on in My Reading

Good Choice! Supporting Independent Reading and Response K–6 by Tony Stead. Copyright © 2008. Stenhouse Publishers.

Appendix T: Response Log for Children in Early Grades

Name: _____ **Grade:** _____

Date	Title	Response	Feelings

☺—I am happy with my response

😐—My response is okay

☹—My response could be better

Appendix U: Response Checklist

Name: _____					Grade: _____			

What Makes a Good Response?

Name of Text									
Response No.	Response 1	Response 2	Response 3	Response 4	Response 5	Response 6	Response 7	Response 8	Response 9
Is my response colorful?									
Did I take time to complete this task?									
Have I put in my best effort with this response?									
Does my response tell the reader about what I have learned?									
Have I included 5–10 amazing or important facts?									
Am I proud of this book response?									
Have I used neat handwriting?									
Is my drawing well designed?									
Have I included enough information?									
Have I checked my spelling?									
Have I checked my punctuation?									
Have I updated my reading response record sheet?									

Appendix V: Response Log for Children in Grades 3–6

Name: _____ Grade: _____

Date	Title	Text Type	Response

Text Type Key: **B**—Biography **I**—Informational **P**—Persuasive **PR**—Procedural **PO**—Poem **S**—Story **E**—Explanation **R**—Retelling **O**—Other

Appendix W: Observation Rubric for Reading Responses

Observation Rubric for Reading Responses Months of: Child's Name: Grade:	Key: 1 Not in evidence 2 Showing signs of 3 Strengthening 4 Nearly always				
Date					
Able to respond to a piece of fiction					
Able to respond to a piece of nonfiction					
Enjoys responding (attitude)					
Is responding in different ways to information read					
The information presented is clear and well organized					
The response is neat and well presented					
Key or important facts and events are presented in the response					
Takes pride in responses					
Able to share responses with peers					
Able to reflect on ways to improve future responses					

Additional Comments

Good Choice! Supporting Independent Reading and Response K–6 by Tony Stead. Copyright © 2008. Stenhouse Publishers.

Appendix X: Organizer for Literature Circle and Book Club Discussions

Likes	Dislikes	Puzzles	Connections

Appendix Y: Literature Circle/Book Club Evaluation

Name: _____ Grade: _____

Date: _____ Name of Book: _____

Group Members:

1. **Did everyone stay on topic?**

   1   2   3   4

2. **Did everyone participate in the conversation?**

   1   2   3   4

3. **Did everyone take turns?**

   1   2   3   4

4. **Did everyone listen to each other?**

   1   2   3   4

How can we make our conversations better next time?

Key: 1—At all times 2—Mostly 3—Sometimes 4—Hardly ever

Appendix Z: Assessment Rubric for Literature Circles/Book Clubs

Observation Rubric for Literature Circles/Book Clubs **Months of:** **Student's Name:** **Grade:** **Independent Reading Level:**	Key: 1 Not in evidence 2 Showing signs of 3 Strengthening 4 Nearly always				
Date					
Able to work cooperatively with other members					
Able to express opinions					
Can listen to others thinking without interrupting					
Able to engage in discussions with informational texts (nonfiction)					
Able to engage in discussions with stories/novels (fiction)					
Accepts others opinions even when they differ from his or her own					
Can take on specific role within the group					
Able to use illustrative sources such as illustrations, graphs, and maps to initiate discussion					
Is aware that his or her thinking may be biased					
Stays on track during discussions					
Makes eye contact with others when speaking and listening					
Able to disagree in a constructive manner without getting personal					

Additional Comments

Good Choice! Supporting Independent Reading and Response K–6 by Tony Stead. Copyright © 2008. Stenhouse Publishers.

Bibliography

Children's Books Cited

Blume, J. 1972. *Tales of a Fourth-Grade Nothing*. New York: Penguin Group.

Carle, E. 1987. *The Very Hungry Caterpillar*. New York: Scholastic.

Magic School Bus Series. New York: Scholastic.

Hirsch, J. 2006. *The Great White Shark*. New York: The Rosen Publishing Group.

Paterson, K. 1987. *Bridge to Terabithia*. New York: HarperTrophy.

Paulsen, G. 1998. *Brian's Winter*. New York: Laurel Leaf.

Pope Osborne, M. 1992. *Dinosaurs Before Dark*. Magic Tree House Series. New York: Random House.

Powell, M. 2006. *Dragonflies Are Amazing*. Markham, ON: Scholastic Canada.

Professional Books

Allen, J. 2000. *Yellow Brick Roads: Shared and Guided Paths to Independent Reading 4–12*. Portland, ME: Stenhouse.

Anderson, R. C., P. Wilson, and L. Fielding. 1988. "Growth in Reading and How Children Spend Their Time Outside of School." *Reading Research Quarterly* 23: 285–303.

Barbieri, M. 1995. *Sounds from the Heart: Learning to Listen to Girls*. Portsmouth, NH: Heinemann.

Booth, D. 2002. *Even Hockey Players Read: Boys: Literacy and Learning*. Markham, ON: Pembroke.

———. 2006. *Reading Doesn't Matter Anymore: Shattering the Myths of Literacy*. Markham, ON: Pembroke.

Brailsford, A., and J. Coles. 2004. *Balanced Literacy in Action*. Markham, ON: Scholastic Canada.

———. 2008. *Booktalk: The Power of Book Clubs in the Middle School*. Markham, ON: Scholastic Canada.

Brailsford, A., and T. Stead. 2007. *Literacy Place for the Early Years*. Markham, ON: Scholastic Canada.

————. 2008. *Moving Up with Literacy Place*. Markham, ON: Scholastic Canada.

Bruner, J. 1986. *Actual Minds, Possible Worlds*. Cambridge, MA: Harvard University Press.

Chaille, C., and B. Britain. 2003. *The Young Child as a Scientist: A Constructive Approach to Early Childhood Education*. Boston, MA: Pearson Education.

Chambers, A. 1996a. *The Reading Environment: How Adults Help Children Enjoy Books*. Portland, ME: Stenhouse.

————. 1996b. *Tell Me: Children, Reading, and Talk*. Portland, ME: Stenhouse.

Clay, M. 1991. *Becoming Literate: The Construction of Inner Control*. Portsmouth, NH: Heinemann

————. 1993. *An Observation Survey of Early Literacy Achievement*. Portsmouth, NH: Heinemann.

Collins, K. 2004. *Growing Readers: Units of Study in the Primary Classroom*. Portland, ME: Stenhouse.

Cullinan, B. E. 2000. "Independent Reading and Social Achievement." *Research Journal of the American Association of School Librarians*. Vol. 3.

Cunningham, P. M., and R. L. Allington. 1999. *Classrooms That Work: They Can All Read and Write*. New York: Longman.

Daniels, H. 2002. *Literature Circles: Voice and Choice in Book Clubs and Reading Groups*. Portland, ME: Stenhouse.

Diller, D. 2003. *Literacy Work Stations: Making Centers Work*. Portland, ME: Stenhouse.

————. 2005. *Practice with Purpose: Literacy Work Stations for Grades 3–6*. Portland, ME: Stenhouse.

Dorn, L., C. French, and T. Jones. 1998. *Apprenticeship in Literacy: Transitions Across Reading and Writing*. Portland, ME: Stenhouse.

Duke, N. K. 2000. "3.6 Minutes per Day: The Scarcity of Informational Texts in First Grade." *Reading Research Quarterly* 35: 202–224.

Duke, N. K., and V. S. Bennet-Armistead. 2003. *Reading and Writing Informational Text in the Primary Grades: Research-Based Practices*. New York: Scholastic.

Fountas, I., and G. S. Pinnell. 1996. *Guided Reading: Good First Teaching for All Children*. Portsmouth, NH: Heinemann.

————. 1999. *Matching Books to Readers: Using Leveled Books in Guided Reading, K–3*. Portsmouth, NH: Heinemann.

————. 2001. *Guiding Readers and Writers Grades 3–6: Teaching Comprehension, Genre, and Content Literacy*. Portsmouth, NH: Heinemann.

————. 2002. *Leveled Books for Readers Grades 3–6*. Portsmouth, NH: Heinemann.

Gee, J. P. 2004. *What Video Games Have to Teach Us About Learning and Language*. New York: Palgrave Macmillan.

Greaney, V. 1980. "Factors Related to Amount and Type of Leisure Reading." *Reading Research Quarterly* 15: 337–357.

Harvey, S., and A. Goudvis. 2007. *Strategies That Work: Teaching Comprehension to Enhance Understanding*. 2nd ed. Portland, ME: Stenhouse.

Hepler, S. I., and J. Hickman. 1982. "'The Book Was Okay: I Love You.' Social Aspects of Response to Literature." *Theory into Practice* 21: 278–283.

Holdaway, D. 1979. *The Foundations of Literacy*. Sydney: Ashton Scholastic.

Hoyt, L. 2002. *Make It Real: Strategies for Success with Informational Texts*. Portsmouth, NH: Heinemann.

———. 2005. *Spotlight on Comprehension: Building a Literacy of Thoughtfulness*. Portsmouth, NH: Heinemann.

Johnston, P. H. 1997. *Knowing Literacy: Constructive Literacy Assessment*. Portland, ME: Stenhouse.

Keene, E., and S. Zimmermann. 2007. *Mosaic of Thought: The Power of Comprehension Strategy Instruction*. 2nd ed. Portsmouth, NH: Heinemann.

Krashen, D. 2004. *The Power of Reading: Insights from the Research*. Portsmouth, NH: Heinemann.

Long, H., and E. H. Henderson. 1973. "Children's Uses of Time: Some Personal and Social Correlates." *Elementary School Journal* 73: 93–199.

McLaughlin, M., and G. L. DeVoogd. 2004. *Critical Literacy: Enhancing Students' Comprehension of Text*. New York: Scholastic.

Miller, D. 2002. *Reading with Meaning: Teaching Comprehension in the Primary Grades*. Portland, ME: Stenhouse.

Morrow, L. M. 1997. *The Literacy Center: Contexts for Reading and Writing*. Portland, ME: Stenhouse.

Ogle, D. 1986. "KWL: A Teaching Model That Develops Active Reading of Expository Text." *Reading Teacher* 39: 563–570.

Organization for Economic Co-operation and Change. 2002. *Reading for Change: Performances and Engagement Across Countries*. Paris: OECD.

Reutzel, D. R., and P. M. Hollingsworth. 1991. "Investigating Topic-Related Attitudes: Effect on Reading and Remembering Text." *Journal of Educational Research* 84: 334–344.

Routman, R. 2003. *Reading Essentials: The Specifics You Need to Teach Reading Well*. Portsmouth, NH: Heinemann.

Rucker, B. 1982. "Magazines and Teenage Reading Skills: Two Controlled Field Experiments." *Journalism Quarterly* 59: 28–33.

Shaffer, D. W. 2006. *How Computer Games Help Children Learn*. New York: Palgrave Macmillan.

Shapiro, J., and W. White. 1991. "Reading Attitudes and Perceptions in Traditional and Nontraditional Reading Programs." *Reading Research and Instruction* 30: 52–66.

Short, K. G., ed. 1995. *Research and Professional Resources in Children's Literature: Piecing a Patchwork Quilt.* Newark, DE: International Reading Association.

Smith, F. 1988. *Joining the Literacy Club: Further Essays into Education.* Portsmouth, NH: Heinemann.

Stead, T. 2002. *Is That a Fact? Teaching Nonfiction Writing K–3.* Portland, ME: Stenhouse.

———. 2003. "The Art of Persuasion." *Teaching Pre K–8* 34 (November/December): 64.

———. 2004. *Time for Nonfiction.* Video/DVD Series. Portland, ME: Stenhouse.

———. 2005. "Comprehending Nonfiction: Using Guided Reading to Deepen Understandings." In *Spotlight on Comprehension: Building a Literacy of Thoughtfulness*, ed. L. Hoyt. Portsmouth, NH: Heinemann.

———. 2006a. *Bridges to Independence: Guided Reading with Nonfiction.* Video/DVD Series. Portland, ME: Stenhouse.

———. 2006b. *Reality Checks: Teaching Reading Comprehension with Nonfiction.* Portland, ME: Stenhouse.

Szymusiak, K., and F. Sibberson. 2003. *Still Learning to Read: Teaching Students in Grades 3–6.* Portland, ME: Stenhouse.

Szymusiak, K., F. Sibberson, and L. Koch. 2008. *Beyond Leveled Books: Supporting Transition Readers in Grades 2–5.* 2nd ed. Portland, ME: Stenhouse.

Taberski, S. 2000. *On Solid Ground: Strategies for Teaching Reading K–3.* Portsmouth, NH: Heinemann.

Vygotsky, L. S. 1978. *Mind in Society: The Development of Higher Psychological Processes.* Cambridge, MA: Harvard University Press.

Weaver, C., L. Gillmeister-Krause, and G. Vento-Zogby. 1996. *Creating Support for Effective Literacy Education.* Portsmouth, NH: Heinemann.

Whang, G., K. D. Samway, and M. Pippitt. 1995. *Buddy Reading: Cross-Age Tutoring in a Multiage School.* Portsmouth, NH: Heinemann.

Zimmermann, S., and C. Hutchins. 2003. *7 Keys to Comprehension.* New York: Three Rivers Press.

Index

Page numbers followed by *f* indicate figures.

A

About Me, 204
About the Author, 209
accuracy, Internet use and, 76
acting, as response, 151–152
advertisements, as response, 173*f*
Amazing Facts I Learned About organizer, 178
Animal Brochure organizer, 191–192
Animal Facts organizer, 177
Apprenticeship in Literacy (Dorn, French, Jones), 25
assessment
    Assessment Rubric for Literature Circles/Book Clubs, 223
    conferences and, 111
    Directed Reading Assessment, 138
    leveling and, 138*f*
    literature circles/book clubs and, 166–167, 166*f*, 167*f*
    responses and, 162*f*
Assessment Rubric for Literature Circles/Book Clubs, 223
atlases. *See* maps
audio formats. *See* media texts
author studies, 31–32, 32*f*, 205
autobiographies, responses to, 170–171*f*

B

bags. *See* book bags
balance, in text selection, 104
baskets. *See* book baskets
behavior, independent reading time and, 6
Benjamin, Lauren, 113
Benson, Katie, 93, 111
Beyond Leveled Books (Szymusiak, Sibberson, Koch), 110, 133
bias, 96*f*
Big Book centers, 26
biographies, responses to, 170–171*f*, 181–182
Biography on organizer, 181–182
Blackwell, Helen, 18
blocking, Internet use and, 72
book bags, 6–8, 7*f*, 9
book baskets, 41–42, 42*f*, 51*f*, 61*f*
book care, 8
Book Changing Schedule, 196
book clubs, 23–24, 163–165, 164*f*, 166, 166*f*, 221, 222, 223
book reports. *See* responses
Book Talk (Brailsford and Coles), 163
Booth, David, 55, 70
borrowing, establishing routines for, 9–10, 10*f*
Brailsford, Anne, 163
Brochure for Parents, 200–203

brochures, 65–66, 65*f*, 66*f*, 173*f*,
    191–192, 193–194, 200–203
Buddy Reading (Whang), 9
buddy reading. *See* partner reading
bulletin boards, 24–25

C

Carle, Eric, 31, 151
Carlo, Jane, 48
Carlson, Mandy, 48, 139
catalogs, 59–60, 60*f*
cause/effect, 96*f*, 185
CDs. *See* media texts
cereal boxes, 60–61
Chambers, Aidan, 163
chanting centers, 28
Character Analysis organizer, 188
Chart Showing Cause and Effect
    organizer, 185
charts, as response, 152*f*, 155*f*, 157*f*,
    173*f*
classroom library
    establishing routines for borrowing
        from, 9–10, 10*f*
    independent reading time and, 6
    magazines for, 57*f*
    for parents, 17*f*
    record-keeping and, 51–52, 52*f*
    as a resource, 39–40
    tracking take home books and,
        19–21, 20*f*
clubs. *See* reading clubs
coding. *See* leveling
Coles, Jan, 163
Collins, Kathy, 110
color coding, 136, 138*f*, 141*f*, 142*f*,
    144–146. *See also* leveling
comfort, independent reading time and,
    5
Comparing Characters organizer, 190
comparisons, 96*f*, 173*f*, 190
comprehension
    independent reading time and, 6

strategies for, 95–96, 95*f*, 96*f*,
    100–101, 100*f*
computer use. *See also* Internet use
    games and, 70–71
    overview of, 69–70
    for pleasure reading, 70
conferences
    implementation procedures for, 116
    individual support needs and,
        120–127
    informal, 114–115
    leveling and, 138
    organization of, 111–112
    overview of, 109–110, 110*f*
    Reading Conference Express,
        113–114, 113*f*, 114*f*
    record-keeping and, 127–132
    sample from grade 2, 117–118
    sample from grade 5, 118–120
    schedule for, 112*f*
    student preparation for, 115*f*
    Teacher's Conference Record Sheet,
        214
    text selection and, 120–121
    traits of, 110–111
    as type of support, 110*f*
confirmation, Reading and Analyzing
    Nonfiction Strategy, 80
content studies
    centers for, 28–30, 29*f*
    independent reading and, 32–35,
        33*f*, 34*f*, 35*f*
    Internet use and, 82–87
    nonfiction and, 45–46
    text selection and, 23, 103–104
contrasting, 96*f*
crossword puzzles, 56
Cullinan, Bernice, 14

D

Daniels, Harvey, 163
Davison, Patty, 74
dePaola, Tomie, 32*f*

del Santo, Doreen, 13

details, 96*f*

difficulty. *See also* leveling

    publishers' assessment of, 145–146

    reluctant readers and, 4

    text selection and, 93–94, 93*f*, 120–121, 138–139

Diller, Debbie, 25

Dinosaurs Before Dark (Osborne), 43

Directed Reading Assessment, 138

directions, 67–68

donations, material shortages and, 53

Dorn, L., 25

DRA. *See* Directed Reading Assessment

Dragonflies Are Amazing (Powell), 124

drawing

    K/1 independent reading time and, 8, 9

    as response, 151–152, 172–176*f*, 183

DVDs. *See* media texts

E

effect, cause and, 96*f*, 185

ELLs. *See* English language learners

emergent readers. *See* approximate grade level

engagement, reluctant readers and, 4

English language learners

    conferences and, 124–125

    home reading and, 16–17

environment. *See also* home

    independent reading time and, 5

    reading places and, 18

    reading the room centers and, 27

evaluation

    comprehension and, 96*f*

    literature circles/book clubs and, 166*f*, 222

Even Hockey Players Read (Booth), 70

expectations, independent reading time and, 5–6, 8

explanatory writing, responses to, 170–171*f*

F

facts, Reading and Analyzing Nonfiction Strategy, 80

feedback, responses and, 154

fiction

    in classroom libraries, 40–41

    informational, 43–44

    responses to, 170–171*f*

fifth grade

    comprehension and, 100–101, 100*f*

    conferences and, 115*f*, 118–120

    leveling and, 142–144

    newspapers and, 58

    Response Log for Children in Grades 3–6, 219

    responses to reading and, 156–160

    text selection and, 98–100, 98*f*, 99*f*

first grade

    author studies and, 31

    Brochure for Parents, 200–203

    classroom libraries and, 42–43, 43*f*, 51

    computer use and, 73

    conferences and, 115*f*

    independent reading time and, 6–9

    leveling and, 136–139

    RAN Organizer for Kindergarten and First Grade, 212

    Reading and Analyzing Nonfiction Strategy, 81*f*

    reading logs for, 13–14, 13*f*

    Response Log for Children in Early Grades, 218

    responses to reading and, 151–153, 152*f*, 153*f*

    student publications and, 62–63

    text selection and, 93–94, 93*f*, 102–103

    tracking take-home books and, 19–20

food boxes, 60–61

Fountas, Irene, 110, 144–145

Fountas and Pinnell leveling system. *See* leveling

fourth grade
    comprehension and, 100–101, 100*f*
    conferences and, 115*f*
    leveling and, 142–144
    newspapers and, 58
    Response Log for Children in Grades 3–6, 219
    responses to reading and, 156–160
    text selection and, 98–100, 98*f*, 99*f*
French, C., 25
fund-raising, material shortages and, 53

G

games, 56, 70–71
Gately, Jennifer, 64
Gee, James Paul, 71
genres, text selection and, 105–108
goal setting, 216
Goudvis, A., 101
grants, material shortages and, 53
Growing Readers (Collins), 110
guided reading, 23
Guiding Readers and Writers (Fountas and Pinnell), 110
Guiding Reading (Fountas and Pinnell), 144–145

H

Hadley, Linda, 137
Harvey, S., 101
home
    Brochure for Parents, 200–203
    opportunities in, 137
    proficiency and, 15*f*
    reading in, 14–19
    tracking take-home books and, 19–21, 20*f*
How to Make organizer, 179
hypotheses, Reading and Analyzing Nonfiction Strategy, 79–80

I

illustrations
    information gathering and, 97–98, 97*f*, 101–102
    K/1 independent reading time and, 6–7, 8
independent reading
    computer use and, 70
    establishing time for, 5–6
    as integral part of reading program, 4
    opportunities for, 23–24
individual support needs, 120–127
info-fiction, 43–44
informal conferencing, 114–115
information gathering, 96*f*, 210
inquiry-based learning, content studies and, 33
intent, 96*f*
interactivity, content studies and, 33
interests
    determining, 47–48, 47*f*, 49*f*
    Survey of Interest, 207
    Survey of Interest for Early Readers, 208
    text selection and, 105
Internet use, 35, 71–76, 82–87, 145. *See also* computer use; media texts
interpretation, 96*f*
Is That a Fact? (Stead), 46

J

Jarrod, Melanie, 112
Joining the Literacy Club (Smith), 18
Jones, T., 25
judgment, 96*f*

K

Keene, Ellin, 127
kindergarten
    Brochure for Parents, 200–203
    classroom libraries and, 42–43, 43*f*, 51

computer use and, 73

conferences and, 115*f*

independent reading time and, 6–9

leveling and, 136–139

RAN Organizer for Kindergarten
and First Grade, 212

Reading and Analyzing Nonfiction
Strategy, 81*f*

reading logs for, 13–14, 13*f*

Response Log for Children in Early
Grades, 218

responses to reading and, 151–153,
152*f*, 153*f*

student publications and, 62–63

text selection and, 93–94, 93*f*,
102–103

tracking take-home books and,
19–20

Koch, Lisa, 110

Krashen, Stephen, 5

L

La Porte, Linda, 6–7

leveling, 14, 133–146, 138*f*, 140*f*, 141*f*,
142*f*

library. *See* classroom library

listening

centers for, 30

K/1 independent reading time and, 8

responses and, 158

listing, as response, 151–152, 153*f*

Literacy Center, The (Morrow), 25

literacy stations, 23, 25–31

Literacy Work Stations (Diller), 25

Literature Circle/Book Club Evaluation,
222

literature circles, 23–24, 163–165, 164*f*,
166, 166*f*, 221, 222, 223

Literature Circles (Daniels), 163

Loeper, Judy, 77*f*

Log of Books and Magazines
Recommended, 198

M

magazines, 56–58, 57*f*

Magic School Bus series, 43

Magic Tree House series, 43

main ideas, 96*f*

maps, 63–65, 145, 180

Marscope, Kay, 19

Martinez, Gabrielle, 56

Mason, Betty, 116

matching, 30–31

material. *See also* text selection

independent reading time and, 5

organization of in classroom libraries,
40–41

selection of, 24

shortages of, 53

media texts, 35, 164

Miller, Peter, 10, 104, 111, 143

mini-lessons

text selection and, 91–92, 92*f* (*see
also* text selection)

as type of support, 110*f*

misconceptions, Reading and Analyzing
Nonfiction Strategy, 80

mobiles, as response, 173*f*

models, as response, 151–152, 173*f*

monitoring

conferences and, 111, 127–132

literature circles/book clubs and,
166–167, 166*f*

responses and, 162, 162*f*

Morrow, Lesley Mandel, 25

motivation

conferences and, 111

encouraging, 17–19

Moynihan, Lisa, 44, 48–50, 120

Mullin, Janet, 93

multimedia. *See* media texts

My Cartoon of Events organizer, 186

My Map of organizer, 180

My Portrait of organizer, 183

N

news boards, 24–25
newspapers, 58–59
nonfiction
    in classroom libraries, 44–46
    content studies and, 34 (*see also* content studies)
    K/1 independent reading time and, 6–7
    leveling and, 135
    responses to, 170–171*f*
notes, conferences and, 127, 128*f*

O

observation
    conferences and, 111
    Observation Rubric for Independent Reading, 215
    Observation Rubric for Reading Responses, 220
Observation Rubric for Independent Reading, 215
Observation Rubric for Reading Responses, 220
On Solid Ground (Taberski), 110
organization. *See also* record-keeping
    book bags and, 6–8, 7*f*, 9
    book baskets and, 7*f*, 41–42, 42*f*, 61*f*
    children's assistance with, 48–50
    classroom libraries and, 40–41
    conferences and, 111–112
    for literature circles/book clubs, 164*f*
    procrastinators and, 125–126
    Reading and Analyzing Nonfiction Strategy, 34, 78–80, 79*f*
    reading binders and, 130*f*
Organizer for Author Study, 205
Organizer for Literature and Book Club Discussions, 221
Organizer for Locating and Recording Specific Information, 210
Organizer for Student Reflection on Selecting Appropriate Texts, 213
organizers, for responding to text, 176–194
overhead centers, 26–27

P

painting, as response, 151–152
pamphlets, 65–66, 65*f*, 66*f*
parents, 16–17. *See also* home
partner reading
    author studies and, 31–32
    centers for, 27–28
    independent reading time and, 6–8, 7*f*
peer recommendations, 103
Perkins, Melissa, 61
persuasive writing
    discussion points and, 58
    responses to, 170–171*f*
Petrose, Laura, 10
photographs, 66–67
pictures, 66–67, 97–98, 97*f*, 101–102. *See also* illustrations
Pinnell, Gay Su, 110, 144–145
Pinnell system. *See* leveling
Place Brochure organizer, 193–194
poetry
    centers for, 28
    responses to, 170–171*f*
point of view, 96*f*
Powell, Marie, 124
Powers of Reading, The (Krashen), 5
Practice with Purpose (Diller), 25
pre-emergent readers. *See* approximate grade level
problem solving, 96*f*
procedural guides, 67–68, 170–171*f*
procrastination, 125–126
proficiency, home reading and, 14–15, 15*t*
puzzles, 56

Q

questions
  independent reading time and, 6
  as response, 154
Quidditch, as analogy, 49–50
quiet, independent reading time and, 6

R

RAN. *See* Reading and Analyzing
    Nonfiction Strategy
RAN Organizer, 206, 211
RAN Organizer for Kindergarten and
    First Grade, 212
read-alouds, 23, 28, 106
reading
  at home (*see* home)
  independent (*see* independent
    reading)
  reluctant readers and (*see* reluctant
    readers)
Reading and Analyzing Nonfiction
    Strategy, 34, 78–80, 79f, 206, 211,
    212
reading binders, 130f
reading clubs, 18–19
Reading Conference Express, 113–114,
    113f, 114f
Reading for Change report, 15–16
Reading Log, 197
Reading Log for Beginning and Early
    Readers, 199
reading logs
  home reading and, 16–17
  as method of record-keeping, 10–14,
    11f, 12f, 13f
  sample, 197, 198, 199
reading the room centers, 27
Reality Checks (Stead), 34, 64, 78,
    95–96, 100
recommendations
  log for, 198
  peer-to-peer, 12, 12f

recordings, as response, 151–152
record-keeping
  classroom library topics and, 51–52,
    52f
  conferences and, 127–132
  Internet use and, 77–78, 77f, 78f
  reading logs and, 10–14, 11f, 12f, 13f
  responses and, 156f, 161f, 162, 162f
  student-based, 130–132, 130f, 131f
  tracking take-home books and,
    19–21, 20f
relevance, 96f
reluctant readers
  conferences and, 121–123
  reasons behind, 4
research
  computer use and, 71–73
  stations for, 33–34
Response Checklist, 218
Response Log for Children in Early
    Grades, 217
responses
  for 3–6, 156–160
  charts as, 152f, 155f, 157f
  checklist for, 159f
  examples of, 172–176f
  ideal frequency of, 150–151
  for K–2, 151–153, 152f, 153f
  literature circles/book clubs as,
    163–165, 164f
  Observation Rubric for Reading
    Responses, 220
  organizers for, 176–194
  overview of, 149–150, 169
  possibilities for, 170–171f
  record-keeping and, 162, 162f
  Response Checklist, 218
  Response Log for Children in Early
    Grades, 217
  Response Log for Children in Grades
    3–6, 219
  responsibility for, 165–166
  sharing of, 154–155, 155f

responses (*cont.*)
    variety of, 155–156, 156*f*, 160–161,
        161*f*
responsibility, student, 165–166
retelling, 96*f*
rhyme centers, 28
rubrics
    literature circles/book clubs, 167*f*
    monitoring, 127–129, 129*f*
    Observation Rubric for Independent
        Reading, 215
    responses, 162*f*

S

scaffolding
    computer use and, 73
    K/1 independent reading time and, 9
    leveling and, 134, 142–143
science, 28–30, 29*f*, 33–34, 33*f*, 34*f*,
    35*f*, 82–85. *See also* content
    studies
sculpture, as response, 173*f*
second grade
    Brochure for Parents, 200–203
    conferences and, 115*f*, 117–118
    leveling and, 141–142
    reading logs for, 13–14, 13*f*
    Response Log for Children in Early
        Grades, 218
    responses to reading and, 151–153,
        152*f*, 153*f*
    text selection and, 93–94, 93*f*
selection, text. *See* text selection
sequencing, 30–31, 96*f*
series books, in classroom libraries, 41*f*,
    43–44
Shaffer, David Williamson, 71
shared reading, 23
shared resources, material shortages
    and, 53
sharing responses, 154–155, 155*f*
shortages, materials and, 53
Sibberson, Franki, 110, 133

Sister Mary Effect, 21
sixth grade
    comprehension and, 100–101, 100*f*
    computer use and, 74
    conferences and, 115*f*
    leveling and, 142–144
    Response Log for Children in Grades
        3–6, 219
    responses to reading and, 156–160
    text selection and, 98–100, 98*f*, 99*f*
small-group work, as type of support,
    110*f*
Smith, Frank, 18
social studies, 32, 85–87. *See also*
    content studies
socioeconomic status, proficiency and,
    15
song centers, 28
sponsorships, material shortages and, 53
Stead, Tony, 46, 64, 78, 95–96, 100
Strategies That Work (Harvey and
    Goudvis), 101
structure, K/1 independent reading time
    and, 9
student publications, 61–63, 62*f*
Student's Individual Goals, 216
summarizing, 96*f*
support needs, 120–127
Survey of Interest, 207
Survey of Interest for Early Readers, 208
surveys
    determining interest and, 47–48, 47*f*,
        49*f*
    Survey of Interest, 207
    Survey of Interest for Early Readers,
        208
synthesis of information, 96*f*
Szymusiak, Karen, 110, 133

T

Taberski, Sharon, 110
Teacher's Conference Record Sheet,
    214

technology. *See* computer use

Tell Me (Chambers), 163

textbooks, content studies and, 33

text features, 96*f*

text selection
    for 3–6, 98–100, 98*f*, 104–105
    conferences and, 111, 120–121
    extension of materials and, 102–108
    independent reading time and, 6
    for K–2, 93–94, 93*f*
    leveling and (*see* leveling)
    mini-lessons for, 91–92, 92*f*
    organizer for, 213
    partner reading and, 27
    student-driven, 24
    text selection and, 99*f*

third grade
    comprehension and, 100–101, 100*f*
    conferences and, 115*f*
    leveling and, 141–142, 142–144
    Response Log for Children in Grades
        3–6, 219
    responses to reading and, 156–160
    text selection and, 98–100, 98*f*, 99*f*

time, providing focused, 4

Time Line organizer, 189

Title organizer, 187

topics
    classroom library organization and,
        41–42, 51–52, 52*f*
    nonfiction organization and, 46*f*
    text selection and, 105–108

turn-taking, 8

V

Very Hungry Caterpillar, The (Carle),
    151–152

videos. *See* media texts

visualizing, 96*f*

visual sources, information gathering
    and, 97–98, 97*f*, 101–102

W

websites, 35, 71–76, 82–87, 145. *See
    also* computer use; media texts

Whang, Gail, 9

work stations, 23, 25–31

writing
    K/1 independent reading time and,
        8, 9
    as response, 149–150, 172–176*f*
    student publications and, 61–63, 62*f*

Z

Zerbo, Katie, 142

Time for Nonfiction
A four-program DVD series

*A chance to actually **see** some of the work Tony describes in **Good Choice!***

This DVD takes us into Lauren Benjamin's first-grade classroom and Lisa Moynihan's third-grade room at the Manhattan New School. As these teachers work with Tony, we see how they set up their classroom libraries and support students with text selection, and we watch students as they respond to their reading in a dazzling array of different ways.

Order this DVD from your local distributor or www.stenhouse.com

In Canada:
www.scholastic.ca

2004
120 minutes
2 discs + viewing guide
ISBN: 978-157110-466-3

Setting Up the Nonfiction Classroom
In a nonfiction classroom, the teacher and the students need to establish the classroom library and give all learners the opportunity to engage with nonfiction as part of independent reading and literacy centers.
- Organizing the classroom library
- Independent reading
- Nonfiction literacy centers

Helping Readers Select Texts: Mini-Lessons and Conferences
If children are to be encouraged to actively select nonfiction as part of their reading lives, they need support to choose appropriate texts. This program explores whole-class demonstrations and individual conferences.
- Providing support in whole-class settings
- Providing support in individual conferences
- Three individual conferences

Whole-Class Mini-Lessons
Students need a variety of demonstrations in whole-class settings to help them as readers and writers of nonfiction. This segment highlights how to gather information and work with persuasive texts.
- Gathering new information in first and third grades
- Small-group instruction: building on whole-class mini-lessons
- Working with persuasive texts

Completing the Jigsaw: Read-Alouds, Visual Literacy, and Responses
This program explores other ways to increase the presence of nonfiction in the classroom. From dressing up as an ant to reading a recipe or baking a cake, these first and third graders' responses demonstrate their love of nonfiction.
- The read-aloud
- Inferring from visual sources
- Responding to nonfiction: first- and third-grade responses

Watch some video clips at
www.stenhouse.com/0466.asp